NO SHELF
REQUIRED

NO SHELF REQUIRED

E-Books in Libraries

Edited by Sue Polanka

AMERICAN LIBRARY ASSOCIATION
Chicago   2011

SUE POLANKA is the moderator of *No Shelf Required,* a blog about the issues surrounding e-books for librarians and publishers. *No Shelf Required* won first place in the academic category of the Salem Press Library Blog Awards, 2010. Her intrigue with e-books began in 1999 with the introduction of NetLibrary and advanced with the evolution of online reference sources. She has been a reference and instruction librarian for twenty years at public, state, and academic libraries in Ohio and Texas and is currently the head of reference and instruction at the Wright State University Libraries in Dayton, Ohio. She has served on the *Booklist* Reference Books Bulletin Advisory Board for ten years, was chair from 2007 to 2010, and writes a column for the Bulletin, "Off the Shelf," to discuss electronic reference issues.

Printed in the United States of America

15 14 13 12 11   5 4 3 2 1

While extensive effort has gone into ensuring the reliability of the information appearing in this book, the publisher makes no warranty, express or implied, with respect to the material contained herein.

ISBN: 978-0-8389-1054-2

Library of Congress Cataloging-in-Publication Data

No shelf required : e-books in libraries / edited by Sue Polanka.
    p. cm.
Includes bibliographical references and index.
ISBN 978-0-8389-1054-2 (alk. paper)
1. Libraries and electronic publishing. 2. Electronic books. I. Polanka, Sue.
Z716.6.N62 2011
025.17'4—dc22

                                                  2010014045

Book cover design by Kirstin Krutsch. Text design in Charis SIL by Karen Sheets de Gracia.

♾ This paper meets the requirements of ANSI/NISO Z39.48-1992 (Permanence of Paper).

ALA Editions also publishes its books in a variety of electronic formats. For more information, visit the ALA Store at www.alastore.ala.org and select eEditions.

for my family

CONTENTS

ACKNOWLEDGMENTS

This book would not have been possible without the guidance and support of some amazing people. First, I thank the contributors: James Galbraith, Jackie Collier, Susan Berg, Shonda Brisco, Amy Pawlowski, Blaise Dierks, Lindsey Schell, Anne Behler, Carolyn Morris, Lisa Sibert, Alice Crosetto, Emilie Delquié, and Rolf Janke. These thirteen individuals provided remarkable content under extremely tight deadlines. Second, I acknowledge Piper Martin and Kathryn Reynolds, my colleagues at Wright State University, for their editorial assistance. Third, I thank Sheila Shellabarger, associate university librarian at Wright State University Libraries, for the freedom to focus my attention on e-books. Finally, I am pleased to recognize the sixteen dedicated individuals in the Wright State University Libraries Reference and Instruction Department. They do their jobs exceedingly well, which provides me the time and energy to read, write, and reflect on the future of e-books.

INTRODUCTION

Why eat a pomegranate when
you can eat a plain old apple. Or
peach. Or orange. When it comes
to fruit and vegetables, only eat
the stuff you know how to grow.

SHERMAN ALEXIE, *WAR DANCES*

The pomegranate is a complicated fruit. Because it is not as commonplace as an apple or orange, many people have never seen, much less tried to open, one. Adventurous souls who do open the pomegranate may be surprised to discover masses of tiny seed packs and not a solid core. Some know to eat the seed pack; others may not. As a result, the pomegranate may be rejected and the more familiar apple or orange selected in its place.

The e-book is complicated, much like the pomegranate. Because it is foreign to many users it may be slighted; users may prefer the more familiar print book, the one they grew up reading. Libraries, publishers, and users question why we should move to e-books when we already have the content in print. When we examine the e-book even more closely, we see masses of business models, formats, and licenses. These aspects are complicated and messy; they may raise questions about the purpose of e-books. Should we remain rooted in our safe, familiar print environment, or should we embrace the challenges inherent in something new?

No Shelf Required: E-books in Libraries offers readers an opportunity to explore the challenges that e-books bring to our libraries and our businesses. It offers innovative ideas on how to integrate e-books into our libraries. It explores complicated issues with e-books in libraries and offers suggestions about how to proceed. This book is an edited work, including contributions from academic, school, and public librarians, faculty, publishers, and vendors. Readers may wish to read the entire work or select chapters. Because chapters are written to stand alone, topics may be discussed more than once, but in different contexts.

We begin our look at e-books in libraries with a glimpse into the evolution of the e-book. James Galbraith provides a colloquial history of e-books in chapter 1. He investigates the various approaches used to create web-based e-books, from Project Gutenberg and the Internet Archive to the International Children's Digital Library. Galbraith also looks into the future of e-books and the commercial and creative perspectives. Finally, he delves into the constantly unfolding Google Books project.

Jackie Collier and Susan Berg discuss the e-book as an emerging tool for learning in chapter 2. Using Brian L. Cambourne's eight principles of learning and the results of the National Reading Panel (NRP) Report, they demonstrate how the e-book relates to the organizational framework of reading instruction. Citing many examples, they correlate the features of four e-book subscription services for emerging readers to the NRP's five areas of focus for reading instruction: phonemic awareness, phonics, fluency, vocabulary, and comprehension. They also acknowledge the challenges educators face using e-books with K–12 learners.

Chapters 3 through 5 discuss how e-books are used in school, public, and academic libraries. Shonda Brisco, Amy Pawlowski, and Lindsey Schell present an overview of the e-book environment in their libraries. They discuss acquiring and licensing, cataloging, and incorporating e-books into the workflow. They also explore access, use, statistics, and marketing, along with benefits and challenges of e-books. Each chapter offers unique perspectives as well. For example, the school library chapter recommends grant resources for K–12 schools; the public library chapter reflects on audiobooks; and the academic chapter discusses sharing e-books across library consortia. As added features, Blaise Dierks spotlights the River Forest Public Library's experience in loaning Kindles in the public chapter, and Anne Behler summarizes the Sony Reader pilot project at Penn State University in the academic chapter.

In chapter 6, Carolyn Morris and Lisa Sibert examine the process of purchasing e-books. They discuss e-book types, business models, and licensing along with library workflow processes like title selection, cataloging, and management of electronic resources. This chapter was written from an academic library perspective, but public and school libraries can benefit from much of the information too.

In chapter 7, Alice Crosetto examines the use delivery reports provided by e-book vendors, focusing on the available data from COUNTER and SUSHI standards. She helps the reader understand and interpret the data that can assist collection development decisions. Crosetto looks into the CLOCKSS, LOCKSS, and Portico programs used for the preservation of digital content.

Publishers and librarians have been concerned about e-book standards for years. Chapter 8, by Emilie Delquié and Sue Polanka, discusses several familiar standards including EPUB, digital rights management (DRM), the ISBN, and digital object identifiers (DOI). Delquié and Polanka look at newer standards like the international standard text code (ISTC) and the Shared E-Resource Understanding (SERU). Some attention is also given to standards that librarians frequently request, especially those governing licensing, pricing, format, and MARC records.

We peer into the future of academic book publishing in chapter 9. Rolf Janke notes the publisher paradigm shift from the print to the digital world. He discusses the economics of e-books and addresses pay-per-view, chapter or article purchases, and free access. Janke also investigates the impact of the e-book reader on academic publishing and concludes with the myriad challenges facing publishers as they move forward.

This book was written in the latter part of 2009. Every attempt was made to ensure currency, but there is no way to stay on top of this subject, for it is constantly evolving. E-books can be complicated and messy like the pomegranate. But if libraries and publishers make an investment in e-books, then we may soon have a library where there is no shelf required.

1

E-books on the Internet

JAMES GALBRAITH

The e-book's day finally appears to be dawning, due to technology improvements, societal shifts and market developments. Today's major e-book proponents will not give up easily, because they see long-term value in the technology and it fits well with their businesses. Quiet progress will lead to eventual success—and perhaps a dominant position—for the e-book in certain segments. One day, paper-based books will be in the minority, but the full transition could take 25 years. (Raskino et al. 2008, 2)

This Gartner Group assessment, written in late 2008, reflects a growing consensus that e-books are finally coming of age. Compared with much current e-book hoopla, the statement is almost somber in its realistic assessment of where e-books are and where they are heading. According to the Association of American Publishers, domestic net e-books sales reached $19.1 million in December 2009, a 119 percent jump for the month. Year-end sales for 2009 reached 169.5 million, a 176.6 percent increase from 2008 (Association of American Publishers 2009). Additionally, a recent *Time* magazine article highlights growing competition in the e-book reader market. As evidence of the market's growth, its author points to Kindle sales of approximately 1.7 million units since the reader's release in 2007 as well as Forester Research's prediction that e-book reader sales would hit 3 million by December 2009 and double to 6 million by 2010 (Rose 2009). The release of Apple's long-awaited iPad, with accompanying iBookstore and iBooks app, adds even more competition, with over 300,000 devices sold on the first day (PR Newswire 2010). These impressive statistics, the high-profile debate over the Google settlement, and recent popular interest in e-books are signs that they have become part of the public zeitgeist.

Yet e-books have taken decades to evolve; Gartner's "quiet progress" is an apt description. Long before Amazon began selling books, before Google began scanning orphaned texts, and before publishers began to "embrace" (in the same way one dances with a porcupine) e-books, thousands of e-books were available to be read and downloaded for free on the Internet. These e-book libraries were the creation of a relatively small but influential e-book community. This community developed core philosophies concerning the preservation of digital e-books, experimented with digitization processes, and learned to cope with accelerating technological change.

In discussing e-books on the Internet, it would be easy to juxtapose the efforts of the early e-book community with the recent so-called crass commercialization of e-books. In this scenario, e-book enthusiasts, academics, and librarians play the Jimmy Stewart role while aggregators, publishers, and distributors play the heavy, perhaps Mr. Potter. The Jimmy Stewart role is a populist role, representing the notion that e-books should be available for free on the Internet in DRM-free format. Mr. Potter is a capitalist, interested in facilitating the discovery of e-books, but only so they can be purchased or accessed through the local library (which pays a premium price for the e-book). Fortunately, the situation is not black and white. The early efforts and the recent commercialization do not have to be in opposition to each other. One is not necessarily better for readers and e-books than the other.

This chapter provides a history of e-books on the Internet and examines the evolution of different philosophical approaches to e-books. It also touches on the future of Internet e-books, from both commercial and creative perspectives. This history is admittedly selective and colloquial, with a few sites serving to illustrate a progression of ideas.

EARLY INTERNET E-BOOK PROJECTS

> Selection by association, rather than indexing, may yet be mechanized. One cannot hope thus to equal the speed and flexibility with which the mind follows an associative trail, but it should be possible to beat the mind decisively in regard to the permanence and clarity of the items resurrected from storage. (Bush 1945)

With these words, Vannevar Bush settled into his argument for a machine—which he called the Memex—that would imitate the human thought process by facilitating nonlinear searching of multimedia resources. Bush's article is celebrated as the first postulation of the idea of hypertext. One could argue that the Internet is the realization of Bush's machine for multimedia searching.

The first Internet e-book was created in 1971. The project, aptly dubbed Project Gutenberg, was the brainchild of Michael S. Hart. Hart, then a student at the University of Illinois, founded Gutenberg on the premise of replicator technology. As Hart put it, "Once a book or any other item (including pictures, sounds, and even 3-D items) can be stored in a computer, then any number of copies can and will be available. Everyone in the world, or even not in this world (given satellite transmission), can have a copy of a book that has been entered into a computer" (Hart 1992). Hart accurately predicted the Internet's power as a syndication tool. Today the phenomenon is well documented, proven every time a music file is downloaded or a new viral video appears on YouTube.

Hart chose the Declaration of Independence as the first document to digitize. Once the document was typed, Hart told his colleagues how to access the file, or sending the 5 kB file to everyone would have crashed the system; six people downloaded the file. Hart had proven his underlying premise. The Gutenberg library was built slowly. In August 1989, Project Gutenberg added its tenth book, the King James Bible. In January 1994, Project Gutenberg celebrated its one hundredth book by publishing the complete works of William Shakespeare. In October 2003, with the addition of the Magna Carta, Gutenberg reached ten thousand volumes. Today, the Project Gutenberg library contains thirty thousand free books contributed by "tens of thousands" of editors (Lebert 2005).

These numbers may seem anemic when one considers the number of books in the Internet Archive or in Google Books. Yet, for nearly four decades, two decades before the World Wide Web, Project Gutenberg has been in the forefront of e-book digitization and collections. Gutenberg first expressed a philosophical basis for Internet e-book collection development policies, in Hart's words "to make information, books and other materials available to the general public in forms a vast majority of the computers, programs and people can easily read, use, quote, and search" (Hart 1992). Gutenberg's mission is elegantly simple: to "encourage the creation and distribution of e-books"; hence the texts are offered primarily in plain text in order to make the e-books as widely accessible as possible.

Project Gutenberg was the first and, for some time, just about the only Internet e-book library. Eventually other libraries went online. In 1985 the classics department at Tufts University began planning the Perseus Digital Library, a digital library of materials on the history, literature, and culture of the Greco-Roman world. Launched in 1987, Perseus was one of the first subject-specific Internet e-book libraries; it has also proven to be one of the most durable.

The Perseus Digital Library's mission is "to make the full record of humanity—linguistic sources, physical artifacts, historical spaces—as intellectually accessible as possible to every human being, regardless of linguistic or cultural background" (www.perseus.tufts.edu/hopper/research). This is a lofty goal, but one tempered with realism: "Of course, such a mission can never be fully realized any more than we can reach the stars by which we guide the twisting paths and blind alleys through the world around us." Perseus's creators believe that, although the ideal is unobtainable, it is everything—"that idealized vision allowed each to change the worlds in which they lived and carry humanity a little farther." In pursuit of these goals, the editors of the Perseus project have expanded the scope of their collections. The site now includes a collection of nineteenth-century American literature and the full text of the *Richmond Times Dispatch*. As of this writing, Perseus stands at over fifty-eight million words of text.

Early efforts such as Project Gutenburg and the Perseus Digital Library were based in a humanist and egalitarian notion of sharing and preserving knowledge, a philosophy shared with the libraries the sites' creators used in their academic studies. Gutenberg adopted something of a "great books" collection policy, concentrating on classics and building a core collection.

Perseus took a subject-specific approach. Both efforts were sustained by a cadre of dedicated individuals.

Early Internet e-book creators faced substantial technical challenges. E-books had to be typed and progress was slow. Early e-book creators viewed one thousand or five thousand books as significant milestones—and they were. It took over twenty-five years for Project Gutenberg to complete its thousandth book: *Dante's Inferno,* added in August 1997. Scanner technology—originally developed in 1957—was not widely available, nor were optical character recognition systems, even though Intelligent Machines Research had introduced the first commercial OCR systems in the 1950s. Eventually scanners and OCR software would change the role of the early e-book creator from typist to editor/proofreader.

Sharing information on the early Internet was not easy. The Internet, advanced for its time, was still clunky. Download speeds were slow, and basic transfer protocols were in their earliest iterations. TCP/IP (Transmission Control Protocol/Internet Protocol) was developed in 1974, after Hart typed his first e-book. Computer use was not ubiquitous. The first Apple computer, the Apple I, was released in 1977, the first IBM PC in 1981. E-book audiences were small, limited to a handful of academics and scientists.

Early e-book creators faced the twin challenges of building collections and learning how best to use new digital technology. Despite these significant challenges, many of the early collections flourished and survive today.

THE WORLD WIDE WEB AND THE EXPANSION OF E-BOOKS

The origin of the Web takes on the aura of modern-day myth when told in its fullness. Unfortunately, we will have to settle for a brief synopsis based on an authoritative account. Tim Berners-Lee wrote a proposal for a World Wide Web in 1989 while working at CERN, the European Organization for Nuclear Research. CERN aggressively promoted the idea, bringing the first web servers online in 1991. In 1994 its promotional efforts culminated in the first annual World Wide Web conference, dubbed the "Woodstock of the Web." Less than one year later, the Web had ten thousand servers and over ten million users. Ultimately, it was the introduction of the Mosaic browser by the University of Illinois in 1993 that opened the floodgates. Mosaic was the first browser to be widely adopted; it opened up the Web to a broad audience (CERN n.d.).

Many of the technical issues faced by e-books creators were resolved with the advent of the Web, a natural platform for e-books that was far more user friendly than BITNET and previous TCP/IP and FTP platforms. With a viable platform in place and a potential audience of millions, academics, libraries, and enthusiasts jumped into digitization projects and the number of e-book libraries began to increase dramatically.

An example of such a site is Renascence Editions, an online repository of works printed in English between the years 1477 and 1799. The site was founded in 1992 by Risa Bear, a staff member of the University of Oregon Libraries (which hosted the site) and an accomplished poetess with a passion for the literature of the period. From 1992 to 2005, Bear and her contributing editors published over 164 e-books on the Web, including works by Shakespeare, Francis Bacon, Mary Wollstonecraft, Edmund Spenser, and Jonathan Swift.

As these libraries grew, people with similar interests began to collaborate and share ideas. E-book communities began to emerge and libraries began to merge. The Luminarium was founded in 1996 by Anniina Jokinen. Initially, Jokinen created the site as a starting point for students and enthusiasts of English literature. The site grew, adding links to similar sites such as Renascence Editions and eventually hosting content shared by colleagues. In essence, the owners of Internet e-book libraries began to do cooperative collection development, often with great success. The process was so easy as to be almost transparent: hyperlink to the other libraries.

One of the best ways to gain an understanding of the excitement of 1993/94 is to read contemporary accounts of the period. One such account was written by Lynn H. Nelson, a professor of history at the University of Kansas. In June 1993, Nelson launched CARRIE, the first full-text history library on the Web. CARRIE was named after the first professional librarian at the University of Kansas. In a brief article titled "CARRIE: A Full-Text Online Library," Nelson gives a firsthand account of the site's launch, which he indicates was an immediate success. Within a month the site had approximately three thousand links to historical texts. Nelson describes receiving enthusiastic letters from people telling him where to find additional texts. One writer sent him a mysterious letter that suggested he "look deep in Colorado State." Nelson searched the site and eventually found a folder called "Stuff." "Stuff" contained three megabytes of socialist texts, including Marx's *Das Capital* and *The Communist Manifesto* (Nelson n.d.).

Despite its success, CARRIE was soon overtaken by other sites. As Nelson writes, "It was only two months until a new day dawned and colleges and universities throughout the country were scrambling to put up World Wide Web sites, and HNSource and CARRIE lost their uniqueness and were overshadowed by the well-funded and professionally staffed projects that began appearing."

Libraries and well-funded projects such as the Library of Congress American Memory project, which grew from a pilot digitization project that ran from 1990 to 1994, were uniquely positioned to develop Internet e-book collections. Aside from their obvious expertise in information management and collection building, they also had the funding and staff necessary to meet the increasing demand for more books, better access models, and more advanced searching tools.

One of the best known of these collections was the University of Virginia Library's Etext Center, founded in 1992. The Etext Center sought "to build and maintain an Internet-accessible collection of documents central to teaching and research in the humanities, and to nurture a user community adept at the creation and scholarly use of these materials." An integral part of the Etext Center's mission was to explore the creation and use of digital collections. A comprehensive list of faculty, staff, and student projects on the center's website (http://etext.lib.virgina.edu/collections/projects/) illustrates the range of the digital projects completed under the aegis of the center; here are just a few of them:

> Shakespearean Prompt-Books of the Seventeenth Century,
>   created by the Bibliographical Society of Virginia
> Witchcraft in Salem Village: The Witchcraft Trials of 1692,
>   by Benjamin Ray, Religious Studies Department
> Absalom, Absalom! Electronic, Interactive! chronology by
>   Stephen Railton, University of Virginia English Department

Many of the projects merged e-texts with other media. The notion that online texts can be enhanced with other media is a natural connection, much like illustrations enhance print books.

As technology improved, projects became more ambitious. In the late 1990s the computer science department at Carnegie Mellon launched the Universal Digital Library (www.ulib.org) "to create a Universal Library which will foster creativity and free access to all human knowledge." The Universal Library's well-known Million Book Project was launched in 2001 with the goal of putting one million free-to-read digital books online by 2007. The scale of the project indicates the incredible advances in digital technology made since 1993. Carnegie Mellon also partnered with governmental and research institutions in India and China. At one point they had over fifty scanning facilities operating worldwide. The Million Book Project met its goal in 2007, scanning approximately 1.5 million e-books. The library holds materials across a broad range of subject areas, everything from Sanskrit literature to technical reports. Twenty languages are represented, including 970,000 works in Chinese, 360,000 in English, 50,000 in the southern Indian language of Telugu, and 40,000 in Arabic (London Business School 2007).

E-book libraries of a similar scale, particularly Internet libraries that offer free e-books, are not common. One that has reached a similar size is the Internet Archive, launched in 1996. The Internet Archive offers "permanent access for researchers, historians, scholars, people with disabilities, and the general public to historical collections that exist in digital format" (www.archive.org). The archive's mission is rooted in the library/archive tradition. It is a visionary effort to create a historical record of a new medium, "to prevent the Internet—a new medium with major historical significance—and other 'born-digital' materials from disappearing into the past." "Born-digital" content included in the archive includes software, audio, video, and e-texts.

As of November 1, 2009, the Internet Archive's Text Collection contained 1,716,115 items. The largest collection, the American Libraries Collection, included 1,139,936 texts. Other collections are Canadian Libraries, 208,867 items; Universal Library, 70,200 items; and Project Gutenberg, 20,377 items. A list of contributors for the American Collection (www.archive.org/details/americana) shows the diverse institutions involved in digitizing books. Contributors include academic and public libraries, the Boston Library Consortium, Lyrasis, and CARLI, the Consortium of Academic and Research Libraries in Illinois. Corporate contributors include

Microsoft, Yahoo! and the Sloan Foundation. Microsoft's contribution alone numbers 339,609 books from its defunct Microsoft Book Search.

The Internet Archive includes an open-source e-book reader. The reader is developed and maintained by volunteers. In a refreshing move, the Internet Archive has an open bug reporting system. Readers can report bugs, view a list of known issues, and even see who has been tasked with correcting each issue.

As a result of the combined efforts of all these individuals and institutions, a prodigious number of e-books are available on the Internet. The collections are as diverse as they are numerous. Aficionados of children's books have many sites to choose from: the International Children's Digital Library, Lookybook, Kids' Corner from Wired for Books, Children's Books Online: The Rosetta Project, Children's Literature from the Rare Book Room of the Library of Congress, and a scan of the *Original Alice,* by Lewis Carroll, in the British Museum's Turning the Pages collection. All these sites are easily found with a search engine.

The Internet also caters to more rarified tastes. Fans of H. P. Lovecraft can read all of his tales of horror at Dagonbytes.com. Readers curious about evolution can browse Darwin's complete works online at the Thackray Medal–winning Darwin Online. Classical music fans might be drawn to the Bavarian State Library's digital library of Felix Mendelssohn's writings. This chapter necessarily fails to do justice to the many e-book libraries available on the Internet; there are too many to document in this article. Suffice it to say, there are many wonderful e-books collections on the Internet waiting to be discovered.

COMMERCIAL E-BOOKS ON THE WEB

All of these efforts at e-book digitization served as a proof of concept for commercial publishers. Still, it was only after the successful transition from print to electronic journals proved the viability and profitability of electronic publishing that publishers warmed to the idea of e-books. Even then, publishers faced several practical issues including digital rights management, the risk of e-book sales undercutting print sales, and finding a suitable electronic format and reader. Many of the early efforts to sell e-books were by aggregators who modeled their databases on commercial journal databases and marketed e-books to libraries.

NetLibrary launched the first e-book database for libraries in 1998. Modeled on journal databases, the platform coupled a discovery interface for finding e-books with a reader for viewing the full text of the e-book. NetLibrary's key innovation was allowing readers to search the full text of an entire e-book library at once. Once an e-book was open, readers could take notes electronically, add bookmarks, link to outside resources, and copy and paste text. Reading from cover to cover was an option, of course, but the emphasis was on research use, similar conceptually to the periodical databases NetLibrary emulated. Within a few years, other e-book aggregators entered into the market, including EBL, ebrary, MyiLibrary, and OverDrive. All these platforms offer similar base functionality, but each has its own unique features as well.

As aggregators were marketing to libraries, other companies sought to break into the consumer market. The history of these efforts is often a study in mergers and acquisitions as opposed to selling e-books. In 1998, Peanut Press began selling e-books online. Peanut Press was subsequently renamed eReader, then after its purchase by Palm was renamed Palm Press. In 2008, eReader (which had reverted back to its earlier name after Palm spun the company off) was purchased by Fictionwise, an e-book company that had formed in 2000. Soon afterward, March 5, 2009, Fictionwise was acquired by Barnes and Noble for $15.7 million. Barnes and Noble has since parlayed this property and its other e-book holdings into one of the largest e-book stores on the Web, with over 500,000 books available.

Individual publishers were a little slower in moving to e-books. The publishers that jumped in most quickly were those successful with e-journals. Notables include Springer and Elsevier, both of which added e-books to their respective proprietary platforms, SpringerLink and Science Direct. The direct-to-consumer market began to open for publishers with the development of affordable e-book readers.

Ultimately, Amazon's Kindle may have the same impact on e-books as Mosaic did on the Internet. The Kindle was not the first reader to market, but it has captured public attention. Amazon, which offers over 350,000 e-books on its website, recently announced plans to sell the Kindle in over one hundred countries. Other companies are competing for the growing market. Sony recently partnered with Google to make over 500,000 books available online. Barnes and Noble unveiled a new e-book reader, the nook, in October 2009. The nook can store and play MP3 files, and it also allows readers to lend electronic books to friends. Apple introduced the iPad and corresponding iBooks app in April 2010. Asustek, maker of Asus netbooks, will soon release its Eee Reader, and Samsung is set to release its Papyrus reader, already available in South Korea, in the United States. Major publishers now sell frontlist e-books direct to consumers. HarperCollins, Random House, Macmillan, Simon and Schuster, and Penguin all offer e-books and downloadable audiobooks online. Publishers are also adding free e-books to the Internet, often as part of promotional campaigns. For example, anyone who has sifted through piles of Harlequin romances in used book stores (or happened to hold a temp job pulping Harlequin novels returned by members of the Harlequin Romance Book Club, as I did) will be touched to know that Harlequin is offering sixteen of its novels for free online in celebration of the company's sixtieth anniversary.

Graphic novel publishers are also getting into the mix. Every week, Marvel Comics offers fifteen free comic books to users who are not ready to subscribe to the Marvel online library, Digital Comics Online. This is a subscription service with over five thousand comics available, including classics like *The Amazing Spiderman*. For those interested in more topical graphic novels, *Slate* magazine's graphic adaptation of the 9/11 Commission's report is available online for free at www.slate.com/features/911report/001.html.

The availability of e-books on both noncommercial and commercial sites coupled with publishers' growing enthusiasm for the direct-to-consumer market is a strong indicator that e-books are reaching maturity on the Internet.

GOOGLE BOOKS

Google's plan to make money from e-books is straightforward. First, digitize as many in-print and out-of-print books as possible, thus creating a massive e-book library. Next, when the inevitable lawsuits are filed, negotiate a settlement with industry associations that sanction your business model and establish a revenue-sharing model that heels your biggest threats. Finally, make gobs of money with your e-book storefront, print-on-demand services, e-book subscriptions to libraries, and advertising revenue. The more complex issue is whether Google's strategy is a good or a bad thing for anyone other than Google employees and the company's shareholders.

In creating Google Books, Google has done an excellent job of building partnerships. Initially, Google partnered with publishers. Among the first to join in were Cambridge University Press, the University of Chicago Press, McGraw-Hill, Oxford University Press, Penguin, Springer, and Taylor and Francis. In December 2004, Google partnered with prominent libraries in launching the Google Print Library Project, subsequently renamed Google Books. Google sought to work with prominent libraries such as Harvard, the University of Michigan, the New York Public Library, Oxford, and Stanford. Eventually other libraries joined in the effort, including the University of California, University Complutense of Madrid, and University of Virginia.

It was the Google Books project—specifically the scanning of the libraries' books—that provoked a lawsuit by the American Publishers Association and the Authors Guild. At the heart of the lawsuit was the assertion that Google had violated copyright law by digitizing dozens of works without the copyright holders' permission. The lawsuit played itself out in a series of increasingly self-serving and tedious pronouncements by both Google and the APA (led by lobbyist Pat Schroeder).

Happily, the parties ran out of things to call each other. In October 2008 they announced a settlement, detailing the key terms in a lengthy (some might say tedious) legal document. Google got the right to scan and display books. For books in copyright, rights holders have to opt in to have their material included; for out-of-print materials, rights holders have to opt out. Google retains 37 percent of the profits from sales of the texts; the remaining 63 percent is divided between the publishers and the authors. The settlement also calls for the creation of a Book Rights Registry. The registry, a nonprofit institution, is to track sales and hold money in escrow for copyright holders until the funds are claimed.

The real fighting began with the settlement. Various organizations including the Internet Archive and the Consumer Watchdog Agency sprang into action, opposing the settlement on the grounds that it would give Google a virtual e-book monopoly. Some of Google's library partners threatened to jump ship. Germany leapt into the fray, arguing that it would give Google the right to scan books by German authors, even though

German authors were not represented in the court proceedings. Finally, the U.S. Department of Justice took notice, launching an investigation of the settlement's potential impact on fair trade.

One might be justified in thinking that perhaps the Google uproar is overdone. The Google Books project will make more books available to readers than ever before. Those books will be easier to find and relatively inexpensive. There is also a built-in safety valve of sorts, for if the experience of the music industry has proven anything, it is that today's tech-savvy consumers will find alternatives to commercial sites if the price is too high or if information is too restricted.

A ruling on the Google settlement from the U.S. District Court in New York had been expected in the fall of 2009; indeed, the first draft of this article expressed the hope that the settlement would at least signal a new act in the dialog about e-books. A complex settlement with such profound implications is hard to negotiate, however. As the date of the settlement came and went, it became clear that the matter would not be settled soon. In February 2010, well after the projected date for a decision, a hearing was held in the Federal Court of Manhattan with many of the participants, including the Justice Department, expressing strong opposition to the settlement even as its proponents strongly defended their interests. More recently, additional lawsuits have been filed, ensuring further litigation. In April 2010 the American Society of Media Photographers filed a class action lawsuit against Google in the U.S. District Court in New York, alleging that Google is displaying copyrighted images from digitized books without properly compensating the artists. The ASMP was joined in this action by the Graphic Artists Guild, the Picture Archive Council of America, the North American Nature Photography Association, and Professional Photographers of America, among others. Also in April, the Open Book Alliance called on the Justice Department to open an antitrust investigation of Google.

Even as the legal argument intensifies, projects are coming to fruition that point out the importance of the Google Books project and the settlement. Most notable is the creation of the HathiTrust. The HathiTrust, a joint project of the CIC and the University of California, is a shared digital repository for all participants' content, including e-books digitized by Google. Although some of the content will be available only to participants, e-books in the public domain will be made available to all, in keeping with the project's goal to "make HathiTrust available, to everyone, anywhere, any time." Should the project stay true to its goal, the result would be a boon to readers.

If the Google settlement is enough to make one want to curl up with a good book (print or electronic), efforts like the HathiTrust offer hope that a solution will be found that advances access to books rather than simply putting them into new commercial silos.

As of this writing, a settlement is still due at "any time."

WHAT ABOUT AUTHORS?

The e-book is still in the early stage of development as a medium. Now that e-book technology is reaching a level of advancement where it does not distract from the text, many writers are no longer content with simply replicating print. Blogs are alive with discussions about multimedia e-books. Writers are experimenting with embedding video, audio, and animation in their work. More engaged authors have already begun to influence the form and the market.

In 2000, Stephen King released his novella *Riding the Bullet* exclusively as an e-book on the Internet. Scribner's servers were so busy that many people were unable to download the work. King had demonstrated that authors (well-known authors at least) could effectively use the Internet to publish their writing. On October 21, 2009, Scribner announced a $35 list price for the e-book edition of *Under the Dome,* Stephen King's latest epic. Evidently, King and Scribner are hoping to prove the point once more at a significantly higher price point.

King's *Riding the Bullet* was a conventional e-book (in terms of its technology, not the text) that was marketed unconventionally. As King was releasing his novella, other authors were working with the medium in less conventional ways. In 1999 the Kennedy Center and RealNetworks launched Storytime Online, a project aimed at using the Internet "to make the unique power and magic of children's books more accessible." Each story featured audio of the authors reading their works combined with visual and textual accompaniment. Stories included Judith Viorst's *Alexander and the Terrible, Horrible, No Good, Very Bad Day;* Debbie Allen's *Brothers of the Knight;* and the poem *Harlem* by Walter Dean Myers. In merging audio, video, and text, the program demonstrated the e-book's potential as a multimedia medium.

The Screen Actors Guild took a similar approach with Storyline Online, which featured members of the Guild reading children's books, with accompanying text and video. Stories on the site include *To Be a Drum,* by Evelyn Coleman, read by James Earl Jones; *My Rotten Redheaded Older Brother,* by Patricia Polacco, read by Melissa Gilbert; *The Polar Express,* by Chris Van Allsburg, read by Lou Diamond Phillips; and *Enemy Pie,* by Derek Munson, read by Camryn Manheim. Sadly, at the time of this writing a note had been posted on the site indicating that funding for the project had run out.

The concept of creating Internet e-books by merging text with Internet technology was taken to another level by writers participating in the Penguin Books project We Tell Stories. We Tell Stories features six different stories from six different authors told over a series of six weeks. Each story incorporates the Internet in the storytelling in a unique way. For instance, Charles Cummings's *21 Steps* uses Google Maps to track the movements of the characters. Each chapter is accompanied by a map of the city of London indicating where the characters are standing. Toby Litt's *Slice* uses a weblog to tell its story. Litt encourages readers to e-mail the characters, and the characters send text messages through Twitter. Nicci French wrote her story *Your Place and Mine* live on the Internet while readers followed along.

Other Internet e-book projects have more of a retro feel. USAToday .com's Open Book series features original works of fiction published in weekly installments, similar to serialized stories published in popular magazines. Although Open Book does not use the Internet as innovatively as We Tell Stories, it takes advantage of the Internet's strength as a syndication tool.

As writers continue to explore the medium, they will necessarily stake out a position in the ongoing debate about a standard file format for e-books. Indeed, they could conspire to render the notion of a single standard obsolete by working across formats as artists might work in a combination of inks, pastels, watercolors, and oils.

A significant change is not likely in the immediate future. Text will remain the most critical element in an e-book, as is appropriate. Moreover, the adoption of the EPUB standard, which supports multimedia functionality, will accommodate most writers' needs. Authors will be able to incorporate video or even sound tracks in their works. Authors/publishers will be able to create so-called deluxe editions of books, just as movie studios have released director's cuts of movies and recording companies have included bonus tracks and video on CD reissues. Soon readers will be able to hear Dan Brown explaining obscure references in *The Lost Symbol* or J. K. Rowling's feelings on how sections of the Harry Potter books were adapted for the screen (clips from the movies could be included to illustrate her points). Successive editions of books will be just as, if not more, desirable than the first edition. Readers will experience books in a very different way than they previously have.

THE FUTURE OF E-BOOKS ON THE INTERNET

The thirty-year history of the e-book on the Internet began with slow and steady development and then launched into accelerated progress. Early efforts focused on putting public domain, rare, and unique content online, in Michael Hart's words, "to make the full record of humanity as intellectually accessible as possible to every human being, regardless of linguistic or cultural background." As the commercial implications of Internet e-books became clear, aggregators and publishers joined in, focusing on the Internet as a market for frontlist titles. Authors became involved too, wrestling with the commercial implications of e-books while exploring them as a new medium. The interests of all those involved are largely complementary. For instance, the digital projects tends to focus on books that are out of copyright, and publishers are concerned about their catalog. All want to promote e-books, even Google Books, which has caused the most legal commotion and disharmony to date.

Some may see something ominous, perhaps ridiculous, in the prospect of Google, large libraries, publishers, computer companies, trade organizations, and lawyers deciding the fate of works they had little hand in creating. Still, there is a possibility that a detente will be forged between these groups, for ultimately they may not have a choice. The Internet's innate utility as a syndication tool is nearly impossible to suppress. Academics and enthusiasts will continue to create websites with free downloadable e-books. Authors will use the Internet as they explore e-books in their literary work. Consumers will make purchasing decisions based on costs (monetary and otherwise). If the costs are too high, independent-minded consumers will find ways to "liberate" e-books by harvesting and sharing the content.

If this situation seems oddly familiar, it is because the digital music industry has just been through a similar process. Happily, good music survived "corporate rock," and the music industry survived Napster. Excellent music was produced under the aegis of large corporations. *Thriller,* the top-selling record of all time, was released by Columbia Records on cassette, LP, and CD; it is currently available in MP3 format on iTunes. Admittedly, good radio was lost along the way, but LastFM and Sirius are proving that the process is reversible.

Today more books are available for readers than ever before; they are also easier to access and less likely to go out of print. E-books are searchable, interactive, and less expensive (millions are free). Writers are exploring the e-book medium and are using it in novel ways. The future of the e-book, and the e-book on the Internet, has never looked brighter.

REFERENCES

Association of American Publishers. 2009. "AAP Reports Publishing Sales Up 4.1% in 2009." Association of American Publishers, February 19, www.publishers.org/main/PressCenter/Archives/2010_February/SalesUp4.1in2009Release.htm.

Bangor Daily News. 2009. "New Stephen King E-Book to Cost $35." October 21, http://www.bangordailynews.com/detail/126117.html.

Bush, Vannevar. 1945. "As We May Think." *Atlantic,* July, www.theatlantic.com/doc/194507/bush#/.

CERN. n.d. "How the Web Began." http://public.web.cern.ch/public/en/About/WebStory-en.html.

Hart, Michael. 1992. "Gutenberg: The History and Philosophy of Project Gutenberg." Project Gutenberg, www.gutenberg.org/wiki/Gutenberg:The_History_and_Philosophy_of_Project_Gutenberg_by_Michael_Hart.

Lebert, Marie. 2005. "Project Gutenberg, from 1971 to 2005." Project Gutenberg, www.etudes-francaises.net/dossiers/gutenberg_eng.htm.

London Business School. 2007. "The Million Book Project—1.5 Million Scanned!" *BizResearch,* November 29, http://lbslibrary.typepad.com/bizresearch/2007/11/the-million-boo.html.

MSNBC. 2009. "Barnes & Noble Unveils New E-book Reader." October 20, www.msnbc.msn.com/id/33401356/ns/technology_and_science-tech_and_ gadgets/.

Nelson, Lynn H. n.d. "CARRIE: A Full-Text Online Library." http://vlib.iue.it/ carrie/carrienelson.html.

PR Newswire. 2010. "Apple Sells Over 300,000 iPads First Day." PR Newswire– FirstCall, April 5, www.prnewswire.com/news-releases/apple-sells-over -300000-ipads-first-day-89904642.html.

Raskino, Mark, Brian Prentice, Bruce Robertson, Jorge Lopez, Martin Reynolds, and Stephen Prentice. 2008. *Emerging Trend: The E-Book's Day Is Finally Ready to Dawn*. Stamford, Conn.: Gartner Group.

Rose, Adam. 2009. "Kindle Killers? The Boom in New E-Readers." *Time,* October 11, www.time.com/time/business/article/0,8599,1929387,00.html.

2

Student Learning
and E-books

JACKIE COLLIER AND SUSAN BERG

How can e-books be used to help students learn, and what do school and public librarians need to know about e-books, current learning theory, and how children learn to read? How can librarians assist teachers and parents to use these exciting new tools for students? Learning is all about thinking and being actively engaged (Calkins 2001), and research has demonstrated that learning to read is a life-altering process (National Endowment for the Arts 2007). As we shift to more digital resources, it is important to consider how e-books can best support student learning and the life-altering processes of learning to read.

Just as it takes a village to raise a child, it takes the collaboration of many individuals to develop motivated learners with the necessary skills to be successful in the twenty-first century. Classroom teachers and intervention specialists are primarily responsible for student learning. This has always been a huge responsibility, but it has become much more stressful with the high-stakes testing and public accountability required by federal No Child Left Behind legislation. Teachers rely on other highly trained professionals to help support their efforts in a variety of ways. Librarians—those in schools and public libraries—are key players in the push to meet the needs of learners in increasingly diverse learning environments. The common goal is to entice diverse students to learn through the implementation of best practices. But how can professionals work together and what role does each play? First, everyone involved needs to build a common understanding of what the research says about best practices and to speak a cohesive language focused on learning theory as it relates to reading.

Students' brains are indeed changing and gravitate to multimedia stimulus to engage them in learning (Caine et al. 2005). E-books are one of the emerging tools for learning that addresses this need for engagement of today's students. Thus, classroom teachers will look to librarians to make connections between the classroom and this technology. In this chapter we review the information needed by librarians and classroom teachers to develop that common language, focusing on meeting student needs. We consider the impact of e-books on teaching reading skills and motivating reading as well as the use of e-reference books and e-textbooks for learning in the content areas.

BEST PRACTICES

Best practices for learning and specifically for reading instruction have been well established in the literature. One major contribution to learning theory literature has been Brian L. Cambourne's (1988) eight principles of learning: immersion, demonstration, engagement, expectations, responsibility, approximations, employment, and response. Cambourne describes his theoretical framework for learning as being a "set of indispensable circumstances that co-occur and are synergistic in the sense that they both affect and are affected by each other" (1995, 184). These eight principles need to be present in best-practices instruction and seem a natural fit for the use of e-books.

E-books can be highly engaging when demonstrations with animation are provided, the use of approximations is promoted as learners try different responses, and feedback on the appropriateness of their responses is offered. As students work with vocabulary selection, puzzles, or even recall questions, they are able to think through their selection, and their approximation is either affirmed or the correct response is given. Thus, their own thinking is validated or corrected. For all levels of learners, these activities support Cambourne's need for response. Learners take responsibility for their learning with e-books when choice is involved; they expect to be successful because they are given control of their responses as they employ problem-solving skills and see what works for them. For example, TumbleBooks, an e-book subscription service discussed later in this chapter, promotes choice and responsibility as students decide whether the book is read to them, the text format moves, or the pacing is altered. These features allow readers to determine how to take responsibility for their own needs as readers.

In the best-case scenario, the e-book can employ all eight of the conditions for learning. So how do teachers and librarians establish the best-case scenario for students' reading needs? Understanding the findings of the National Reading Panel on scientifically based reading instruction is a strong beginning to addressing that question.

In 1997 the U.S. Congress convened a group of scholars to examine the research on best practices in reading instruction and to find the patterns of success in order to better inform educators. The result of this effort is known as the National Reading Panel Report (NRP 2000). The panel determined that there are five areas of emphasis and specific findings within the area of reading that should guide instructional decision making in the area of reading instruction. Their findings from the examination of the research provide a foundation for the teaching of reading termed "scientifically based reading instruction"; in other words, the methodologies are supported by the findings of the NRP.

The five areas of focus as determined by the NRP are phonemic awareness, phonics, fluency, vocabulary, and comprehension. These five areas are now the organizational framework for reading instruction. Each of these areas has specific findings that support best practices in the teaching of reading at any developmental level. For librarians and classroom teachers seeking ways to promote literacy with students of all ages and all levels of development, these are important common threads of information. E-books can be used to promote these five areas of focus.

Phonemic awareness and phonics are about the sounds of our language and the letters representing those sounds. This is important because it provides the foundation for later reading and writing as students take their understandings to print. Read-aloud books or book pages that highlight text as it is being read, such as used in Scholastic's BookFlix, help make the connection between oral and print language. Matching the picture to the beginning sound and the letter that represents that sound uses digital technology to support emergent readers. The panel found that this level of reading instruction is best delivered in small groups, at a variety of ages, and that student manipulation of letters and sounds is highly effective. Instructional tools, such as the range of e-books presented here, that promote student engagement in working with different sounds and their representations are positive examples of how the findings of the NRP can be supported.

A third area of NRP focus is fluency—that is, reading orally with speed, accuracy, and prosody (proper expression and timing). The research findings explain that guided oral reading and also repeated reading support building fluency. E-books promote reading fluency when they are so engaging that students want to revisit them, or when students are able to return easily to the text and repeatedly read a selection.

Vocabulary, with a long history of research on its relevance to successful reading, is the fourth area of NRP findings. The panel determined that both oral and print vocabulary are important to the success of good readers and should be a focus of instruction. The NRP found that students who read more have larger vocabularies and benefit from being exposed to words multiple times, in multiple settings, and in varying ways. Teachers can promote extensive reading by using tools such as those found in BookFlix's Read the Book. This e-book format promotes both the oral and visual interaction with text and is highly engaging, so it supports student vocabulary growth.

The fifth area of focus for the NRP is comprehension—intentional thinking that leads to meaning as the reader interacts with the text. This vital part of the act of reading is a large area of concern for teachers. It is the meat to the bones of decoding and requires engagement and problem solving on the part of the reader. The NRP analysis found that several instructional methods worked well for teaching reading comprehension. Students must be asked questions and taught to self-monitor, to use aids such as graphic organizers, to determine text structures, and to summarize as they read.

Librarians and teachers must work together to determine how e-books can play a part in the implementation of NRP recommendations and best practices in learning theory. Librarians add value to the learning process by making classroom teachers aware of the availability of e-books and suggesting and modeling ways that they can be used in the classroom or at home. By explicitly pointing out ways in which e-books can be used to build phonemic awareness, phonics, fluency, vocabulary, and comprehension, librarians become credible instructional partners to the classroom teacher. They also become leaders in the school's literacy and technology initiatives.

E-BOOKS FOR EMERGING AND DEVELOPING READERS

Four subscription services for beginning readers that librarians should investigate are BookFlix, TumbleBooks, Big Universe, and the International Children's Digital Library. Though similar in some ways, each service has particular strengths that can support NRP scientifically based reading instruction (table 2.1). Librarians can review these and other services and work with classroom and intervention teachers as well as curriculum staff to select the best resources for their school. They can also provide staff development and support for teachers and promote home use through the library website and parent workshops. Often funding sources outside the regular library budget can be found to purchase e-books. When tied to NRP findings, textbook funds and grants become real possibilities.

Scholastic's BookFlix is an innovative online literacy resource that pairs fiction books with nonfiction books for grades K–3. This is support for teachers who are working to help children understand how information is presented differently in different genres, supporting one of the findings for text comprehension of the NRP. The fiction titles are classic Weston Woods–produced video storybooks—many of these Caldecott winners are familiar to most librarians who work with children. The nonfiction titles are e-books with a variety of reading assistance options. The imaginative pairings include *Harry the Dirty Dog* (Zion)/*Keeping Clean* and *Hansel and Gretel* (Marshall)/*We Need Directions!* Twenty-one of these pairs are available in Spanish.

Children can choose to turn read-along on or off while watching the video of the fiction title. Words are highlighted as spoken by the narrator, building fluency and word knowledge. The NRP found that paired reading (reading along with someone to model pacing) and visual acuity (noticing

Product	Picture books	Fiction books	Hi/lo titles	Instructional features	Award books	Video	Audio	Animation	Free	Individual subs	Foreign languages	Create books
Big Universe www.biguniverse.com	X			X					X*	X	X	**X**
BookFlix http://teacher.scholastic.com/ products/bookflixfreetrial/	X			**X**	**X**	**X**	**X**				X†	
International Children's Digital Library http://en.childrenslibrary.org	X	X					X*			**X**	**X**	
TumbleBooks www.tumblebooks.com	X				X	X		X	**X**		X	
TumbleReadables www.tumblebooks.com		X	**X**	X			X					

Table 2.1 *Four E-book Resources for Beginning Readers*

X = has this feature   **X** = strength of this resource   * = limited   † = Spanish only

the features of a word) both support the needs of developing readers. Students who need to develop both oral and visual word knowledge are supported, and so both visual and auditory vocabularies are strengthened. The video can be enlarged, which is a great option for teachers to use for whole-class viewing on interactive whiteboards, but it can also be a tool of individual differentiated learning with struggling or advanced readers, as students build independence and become comfortable with the use of the technology (Tomlinson 2004).

Another option allows children to click on yellow highlighted words so they can read and hear definitions to build vocabulary, again supporting the NRP focus on visual awareness of words. When they select a read-along feature, the book is read aloud and words turn red as they are spoken, which also supports the paired reading that the NRP found successful. This feature encourages children to follow along, strengthening multiple skills while keeping them engaged. Audio level can be controlled but not speed. Students can first read the e-book with the read-along feature turned on, then go back and read independently. They can repeat the process to reinforce letter and word recognition (phonics), word usage (vocabulary), and flow of reading (fluency).

For each pair of books, additional activities and resources support individual or group needs. For children there are Puzzlers (interactive games to assess vocabulary, distinguish between fact or fiction, or practice sequencing), Meet the Author (with links to the author's website), and Explore the Web (high-quality, annotated website links to extend the topic). For teachers there are lesson plans aligned to national standards—science or social studies as well as language arts.

There are additional support features for teachers, parents, and librarians. Most important is the ability to sort by reading level (lexiles 20–750) or Reading Counts (Scholastic's reading/quiz software program similar to Accelerated Reader). In this way teachers can support the NRP finding that there must be a strong match between students and their use of instructional and independent levels of texts.

BookFlix is a terrific resource for building children's background knowledge and helping them become fluent independent readers. It is clearly designed with instruction in mind, using key principles of what we know about early reading. Scholastic has online funding suggestions and alignment guides. School or library subscriptions come with off-site access.

Another online subscription service with specialized learning features is TumbleBooks, which includes animated audio e-books for K–3 students. The picture books are from a variety of mainstream publishers, with some popular titles but fewer award winners than BookFlix. Readers select a picture book from categories such as holidays, friends/family, school, numbers/letters, or health/safety. The first thing the user notices when reading a book on TumbleBooks is that the printed page is animated. Sometimes the page is simply panned (e.g., moving from the bottom of the page to the top). More often, elements on the page move or appear on the screen at different times. This is a good example of what Gralley (2006) described as taking advantage of features of the new digital medium when creating e-books rather than just transferring the printed page to the screen. The entertainment value certainly increases (and student engagement), but these features could be distracting for struggling readers and children with learning disabilities unless used wisely (perhaps as support with a para-professional). In their research on CD-ROM storybooks, DJong and Bus found that the "many attractive options of electronic books seem to divert children's attention from text and number of readings of the text in favor of iconic and pictorial explorations" (2002, 154). Students with specific learning needs can use e-books successfully, but adaptations of how they are used should be considered.

The reader has several controls—including audio, auto, and manual—that can be used in combination. In auto mode with the audio turned on, the story is narrated aloud. Whole sentences (rather than word by word, as in BookFlix) turn red as they are read. This helps young readers or older readers with emerging skills hear a model of the prosody of fluent reading, highlighting appropriate expression and the continuity of words rather than the word calling associated with decoding alone. The NRP states that the purpose of reading is to understand a message, so anything that can move emergent readers away from word calling to comprehension of the message is valuable. The auto mode of TumbleBooks promotes such an understanding by allowing sentences and passages to be seen as a whole instead of a series of parts (words).

When the book is read in auto mode with the audio turned off, the pages still turn automatically, helping students experience appropriate pacing of the text. In manual mode, the reader controls the timing, but sentences still turn red, one at a time. For struggling readers this encourages fluency and a holistic view. Distractibility issues can be minimized if an adult or more mature reader works one-on-one with the student.

Some recently added books have a word help feature in which more difficult words are highlighted in yellow and have an audio icon. When a child clicks on it, the word is pronounced, sounded out syllable by syllable, then pronounced again. This feature supports the NRP findings on phonics awareness, for words are broken down into parts and vocabulary words are visually highlighted and pronounced. For the learner there is immediacy to the response, supporting Cambourne's learning theory. Unlike BookFlix, TumbleBooks does not give a definition, which must be provided separately if needed.

Additional educational features include puzzles and games, some with more educational value than others. With the school subscription, students can write book reports using the book report tool by answering a series of generic questions. The NRP found that questioning is a key component of building text comprehension. The questions are valuable if they are generated by others (in the case of the questions about main characters or quizzes) but also if they are generated by the reader (such as a review-of-your-work feature). Quizzes for each book ask five multiple-choice questions at the knowledge and comprehension level. When the quiz is completed, the score is given ("your total score is 2/5"), which provides immediate feedback. Tools for teachers are limited, but the website can be viewed in French and Spanish, which is a teacher resource for English-language learners—a growing classroom concern.

TumbleBooks is an ambitious e-book subscription service. Along with its companions TumbleReadables (for older readers) and TumbleTalkingBooks (audiobooks), it is marketed exclusively to schools and libraries. A variety of subscription options are available, with home access as part of the deluxe school and library subscriptions. Nonfiction titles are being added. These are all great benefits, but they are strengthened by the support of an education-ally sound rationale of how these electronic resources promote best practices.

A third online subscription service is Big Universe, with e-books from book publishers as well as a highly developed write-your-own-book fea-ture. Some books are available in several languages; most titles are not well known or award winners. Besides fun picture books there are basic curriculum-based nonfiction works for younger readers and some illustrated classics, biography, and graphic titles (Saddleback Educational Publishing) for older readers.

None of the site's books have enhanced features such as audio, dictio-nary, or bookmarking, although books can be searched by age, category, language, or keyword. Overall, Big Universe does not go much beyond merely placing print books online, and its offerings are not as grounded in learning best practices as BookFlix or TumbleBooks. The strength of Big Universe is its utility for students to create and publish their own books. Students can easily write and design a book that looks quite professional (with the added bonus of saving, printing, and sharing capabilities), so this option supports the connection between writing and reading. With proper support the e-book site can be used to transfer a learner's oral vocabulary to a written vocabulary. Teachers or parents focusing on social or emo-tional issues can use this feature to create personalized books, including uploaded personal pictures. For example, intervention specialists can make social storybooks showing positive behaviors with scenes from the child's school and classroom.

Although Big Universe e-books are not written and illustrated by well-known children's authors and illustrators, the enhanced reading features along with the writing and publishing opportunities make it a very useful e-book resource. Future plans include adding reading levels (e.g., Fountas and Pinell), which supports the NRP finding that students should be reading text at their "just right" level. Additional new features are to include after-book activities, an improved book search, and the ability to order a bound print version of member-created books. It is also working to add publishers.

New subscription-based e-book sites continue to be developed. Named a "Top 10 Digital Resource" by *School Library Journal* in 2009, One More Story is an attractive and simple-to-use site featuring award-winning picture books with a read-aloud option. Books are professionally narrated with original music.

Not all web-based e-book sites are fee based. The International Children's Digital Library (ICDL) is an ambitious research project with the goal of making more than ten thousand books in at least one hundred languages freely available over the Internet. At the core of this project is the belief that cross-cultural understanding is enhanced when children learn more about the similarities and differences of the world's cultures. The Human-Computer Interaction Laboratory at the University of Maryland and the Internet Archive are building this library and investigating how children search, browse, read, and share books in electronic form. Using rotating teams of children ages six through eleven, the researchers have involved children in the development of the site's design and technology. Research papers and videos explaining the project are available on the website, stimulating learners who have strong literacy skills and can benefit from high-end differentiation. These learners (at school and at home) require authentic purposes to engage and motivate them to use their advanced skills effectively.

The ICDL collection includes only books that have originally been published in print format and for which ICDL had obtained copyright permissions. Books are published in the original language. If they have been physically published in more than one language and ICDL has permission for other versions, then multiple language versions are made available.

The website itself can be viewed in many different languages, with most translation being done by volunteers.

The site has many unusual and helpful features. For example, small collections of books have been assembled on themes that promote important aspects of multicultural understanding: celebrating differences, overcoming challenges, friendship, seasons, strong women, and water as an essential resource. This feature should be helpful for teachers integrating the language arts curriculum with science and social studies. Since children assist with the project, the site offers search criteria that use terms children would use in their everyday lives, such as "make believe" for fiction and "true" for nonfiction. Additionally, several of the books have an accompanying audio file, which is opened as a separate file as the reader is signaled to advance the page by a tone. In this way, young readers can support their fluency skills by having the reading modeled for them.

ICDL is an exciting site to use in the classroom to promote global understanding. One of its strongest uses is with students for whom English is not the first language. Where else can teachers find books in fifty languages from Afrikaans to Yiddish? Children will love being able to read a story in its original language. Perhaps they could share the story with their class, with the book projected on a large screen or interactive whiteboard. Foreign-language classes could read titles in the language they are studying and create podcasts reading the book aloud. They could also work in teams to translate the text into English.

E-BOOKS FOR OLDER STUDENTS

The goal for older students is to motivate them to read often and widely. The digital generation values online activity and spends a great deal of time connected to the Internet and to each other. E-books give librarians another tool to motivate students to want to read. Some students may enjoy reading on their preferred device, whether it is a laptop, cell phone, or MP3 player. Fiction and nonfiction recreational reading of e-books offers new opportunities for social interaction. As library catalogs allow for reader's comments and fans of genres and authors meet online, the digital generation has more opportunities to connect with each other and with reading. It is not hard to imagine electronic versions of blockbuster series like Twilight or Harry Potter being read on iPods with options for sharing comments, reactions, and speculation with other readers in real time. Teachers could use this type of feature for dialog and discussion of literary criticism, both ways to support comprehension according to the NRP. The concept of choosing alternative story paths as previously popularized in print series such as the Choose Your Own Adventure books can easily be used in e-books.

Besides e-books selected and purchased by libraries and distributed through library catalogs, there are online subscription services for fluent readers similar to those discussed above for emerging and developing readers. TumbleReadables includes text versions and read-alongs of early readers, chapter books, middle school titles, teen titles, children classics, and adult classics (including Shakespeare). Many but not all TumbleReadables titles are read-alongs. The audio component can be turned off and the book read manually if desired, so there is the option of scaffolding for the reader. There are some features for struggling readers. The text turns red, sentence by sentence, as it is read, so students can have support for word recognition skills (a foundational piece of vocabulary knowledge). Books that have no audio component do have the feature of controlling the timing of the page turns. This could be used to improve fluency if it is not confusing to the reader and can be turned off in manual mode. The audio is from well-produced audiobooks and includes music and sound effects. Teachers might bookmark passages and play them to the class to promote discussion, a teaching strategy promoted by the findings of the NRP. Additionally, text size can be increased for students with vision problems, and some books have quizzes in the same format as TumbleBooks.

E-REFERENCE BOOKS

School libraries, especially high schools, are having success using e-books for reference. High-quality reference sources are essential for learning in all content areas. Whether it is science, social studies, language arts, math, health, or the fine arts, there are e-reference books that provide credible, well-written, well-documented information in a format that often is preferred by students.

There are many advantages to using e-reference books, including improved access to the information in these books. With licensing agreements such as offered by the Gale Virtual Reference Library, several students can use the same e-book at the same time during class visits to the library. Students gain 24/7 use of titles that in print may be for library use only or overnight checkout. Ease of use in e-reference books is enhanced with topics listed on drop-down menus and keyword searching. Students can take notes by highlighting and copying and pasting text and graphics to word processing files. Of course, this advantage brings one of the greatest difficulties. Students tend to copy or print first and read and comprehend later. Teachers and librarians need to do a lot of work with students to ensure that original work and critical thinking take place.

E-TEXTBOOKS

Textbooks are traditionally a reading challenge for any student who struggles with decoding and or comprehension. Textbooks are frequently written at a text level that exceeds the independent reading level of students. As e-textbooks evolve and include more integrated learning enhancements, they have real potential for improving learning. Higher education has been the leader in the use of e-textbooks, though California just began a huge initiative to use more online learning materials including open-source textbooks in K–12. The driving factor has not been improving learning but rather reducing cost, as concern has been mounting over the high cost of textbooks. The typical college student spends up to $1,000 per year on textbooks, and e-textbooks can reduce this cost by half or even more (Rickman et al. 2009). Typically e-textbooks have been digital equivalents of print titles, so improved learning cannot be expected. Indeed, in a study of a campuswide textbook initiative at Northwest Missouri State University (Rickman et al. 2009), 60 percent of the students reported that they read more when using print textbooks than when reading e-textbooks. Students preferred e-textbooks only when cost savings was a factor.

A significant feature of any e-textbook is the capacity for text-to-speech, that is, having the textbook read aloud. This may be done through screen reader software already used on a computer or through software that is part of the e-textbook. This is a critical accommodation for students with limited vision or reading disabilities. Other techniques for improving readability for learners with specific reading needs include making the font larger, adding highlighting, or changing the contrast between the text and the background. Part of the screen can be blocked out to reduce distractions. Teachers can build accommodations to assist special needs students, including concept maps, notes, and increased spacing between words. Cavanaugh gives an excellent review of techniques for making a book more accessible to special needs learners in *The Digital Reader: Using E-books in K-12 Education* (2006).

The next generation of e-textbooks is likely to be much more than digital versions of print books. Some e-textbooks today already have some enhanced features that may improve learning, such as these:

- Built-in dictionaries and pronunciation guides
- Bookmarking
- Keyword searching
- Annotating/highlighting
- Shared notes
- Read-aloud
- Links to recommended readings/websites
- Multimedia (video, audio, animation)
- Interactive simulations/games
- Learning assessment tools (e.g., quizzes)
- Integration with online course management systems (e.g., Blackboard)

These features support Cambourne's eight principles of learning. Links to websites, primary sources, and recommended reading often are available on companion websites for print textbooks; these links may be used more when they are integrated into the electronic text. The biggest opportunities for increasing learning may be through integrated multimedia. Audio and video segments of experts speaking or demonstrating concepts can bring textbooks to life. Animated graphs or diagrams can make processes clearer by engaging a variety of learning modalities. Interactive learning activities including simulation games can bring the power of social networking to classroom learning. Assessment tools such as self-check quizzes may aid students with metacognition strategies, supporting the NRP's finding for ongoing assessments and learning theory's focus on approximation and feedback. Indeed, e-textbooks with these attributes blur the line between what has been called courseware and what has been called an e-textbook.

Textbook publishers' plans certainly indicate that we can look forward to richer, more involved learning features. Six of the largest higher education textbook publishers formed an alliance in 2007 called CourseSmart to offer digital versions of their textbooks, greatly improving higher education e-textbook availability. An emerging standard for e-textbooks, Common Cartridge allows content to be moved more freely into and out of major course management systems (e.g., Blackboard, Desire2Learn). It goes beyond portability of text to include learning assessment tools, learning objects, and interactive capabilities (Nelson 2008). Full integration with course management systems is critical as colleges continue to develop online courses.

Open-access digital textbooks are an intriguing option (Polanka 2010). They are free—developed by authors and educators for educational purposes. Creative Commons licenses permit copying, sharing, and changing as long as the original author is credited. Instructors can select content, edit content, and make new content. Customized texts can be created and distributed electronically or printed. A great resource for K–12 schools is CK 12 Foundation, a nonprofit organization with the mission of reducing textbook costs. It uses a slick web-based collaborative model called FlexBooks. The initial focus is on science and math content.

Connexions, Flatworld Knowledge, and Merlot are higher education open-source textbook sources. Connexions, from Rice University, was founded in 1999 and includes thousands of "knowledge chunks"—modules of educational material covering multiple disciplines. It includes an authentication feature similar to peer review called "Lenses." Some content is also appropriate for K–12 schools. Flatworld Knowledge textbooks also cover multiple disciplines. Faculty can select existing textbooks or remix content to create their own. Students can read free online or choose from various fee-based downloading options. A social networking option adds value, allowing students to interact with other students using the same text. Merlot contains much more than textbooks. Quizzes, tutorials, case studies, and assignments in many disciplines are included. Merlot was created in 1997 at California State University and features peer review by an editorial board.

School librarians have an opportunity to integrate library materials with open-source textbooks. In an editorial in *School Library Journal,* Brian Kenney suggests that the "digital textbook could be media specialists' Trojan horse, stealthily moving materials from the library to the classroom" (2009, 9). He suggests that links to database articles, streaming media, and library books (both printed and e-books) can help address diverse learning styles and provide access to different viewpoints.

CHALLENGES

Although the potential for e-books to improve learning is great, there remain some serious questions and issues. Not all learners have up-to-date computers and high-speed Internet access at home. Neither do all schools. Public libraries can play an important role in providing access to equipment and subscribing to e-book services. School libraries may need to find ways to offer extended hours to supplement access for students who lack it at home.

E-books are still in a transitional state. There are still format issues to sort out. Not all books that young people want to read are available digitally. The hardware for using K–12 e-textbooks on a large scale is not in place. Electronic reference books are clearly preferred by young people, but many teens still prefer to read for pleasure on pages rather than screens. The time is probably coming when digital will replace print, but efforts like the one at a school in Massachusetts are clearly premature. Media reports indicate that this private academy is replacing a twenty-thousand-book library to go completely digital. Students can borrow eighteen digital readers (Kindles) to read titles purchased from Amazon.com, or they can read free books available on the Internet on their laptops. Unfortunately for the students, most of these free books are classics, scholarly tomes, or old out-of-copyright titles—not the latest books by popular authors teens want to read. Books that truly unite text and illustrations, such as many of the winners of the American Library Association's Sibert Award for distinguished nonfiction, are not available electronically. Research on free voluntary reading conducted by Stephen Krashen (2004) and others clearly shows that students need books that they find so compelling that they want to read more. This means access to the widest possible variety of genres and formats. E-books are part of a library, not a complete solution.

A final concern requires consideration. Cognitive neuroscientists are beginning to look more deeply into what digital immersion will mean to learners, especially young children. This chapter focuses on the many ways e-books can enhance learning, but questions remain about how the new media affect child development. Will young children learn to go deeper into the text to really think about what they are reading, or will they be distracted by links, sidebars, and multimedia? Learning is not passive; learners must stop and think about what they have read, make connections to what they already know, and construct their own meaning.

SUMMARY

E-books clearly offer new opportunities for improving student learning. For beginning readers, features unique to e-books support research-based best practices as identified by the NRP and Cambourne's theory of learning. A variety of subscription services are available, each with its own strengths. Special learners, whether they are English-language learners, reluctant readers, at-risk readers, or special education students, can benefit from e-book features such as text to speech, multimedia, note taking, and highlighting. Digital resources also appeal to the digital generation by keeping them engaged, allowing them to try one response and get immediate feedback and take responsibility for their learning. Librarians can lead in the use of these new tools by collaborating with classroom teachers and connecting best practices to e-book use. They play a key role in helping learners prepare for successful lives in the twenty-first century by linking the human resources (supported by knowledge of scientifically based reading instruction) to new tools for the purpose of supporting student needs.

REFERENCES

Caine, Renate Nummela, Geoffrey Caine, Carol McClintic, and Karl J. Klimek. 2005. *12 Brain/Mind Learning Principles in Action.* Thousand Oaks, Calif.: Corwin Press.

Calkins, Lucy McCormick. 2001. *The Art of Teaching Reading.* New York: Longman.

Cambourne, Brian L. 1988. *The Whole Story: Natural Learning and the Acquisition of Literacy.* Auckland, N.Z.: Ashton-Scholastic.

———. 1995. "Toward an Educationally Relevant Theory of Literacy Learning: Twenty Years of Inquiry." *Reading Teacher* 49 (3): 182–188.

Cavanaugh, Terence W. 2006. *The Digital Reader: Using E-books in K-12 Education.* Eugene, Ore.: International Society for Technology in Education.

De Jong, Maria T., and Adriana G. Bus. 2002. "Quality of Book-Reading Matters for Emergent Readers: An Experiment with the Same Book in a Regular or Electronic Format." *Journal of Educational Psychology* 94 (1): 145–155.

Gralley, Jean. 2006. "Liftoff: When Books Leave the Page." *Horn Book Magazine* 82 (1): 35–39.

Kenney, Brian. 2009. "As Goes California: A Flawed Initiative Becomes a Fabulous Opportunity." *School Library Journal* 55 (9): 9.

Krashen, Stephen. 2004. *The Power of Reading: Insights from the Research.* 2nd ed. Westport, Conn.: Libraries Unlimited.

National Endowment for the Arts. 2007. "To Read or Not to Read." Research Report 47 (November), www.nea.gov/research/ToRead.pdf.

Nelson, Mark R. 2008. "E-books in Higher Education: Nearing the End of the Hype?" *EDUCAUSE Review,* March/April, www.educause .edu/EDUCAUSE+Review/EDUCAUSEReviewMagazineVolume43/ EBooksinHigherEducationNearing/162677.

NRP National Reading Panel and National Institute of Child Health and Human Development. 2000. Report of the National Reading Panel. *Teaching Children to Read: An Evidence-Based Assessment of the Scientific Research Literature on Reading and Its Implication for Reading Instruction.* Washington, D.C.: NRP.

Polanka, Sue. 2010. "Off the Shelf: Exploring Open Access E-Textbooks." *Booklist* 106 (16): 69.

Rickman, Jon T., Roger Von Holzen, Paul G. Klute, and Teri Tobin. 2009. "A Campus-Wide E-textbook Initiative." *EDUCAUSE Quarterly Magazine* 32 (2), www.educause.edu/ EDUCAUSE+Quarterly/EDUCAUSEQuarterlyMagazineVolum/ ACampusWideETextbookInitiative/174581.

Tomlinson, Carol Ann. 2004. "Differentiation in Diverse Settings." *School Administrator* 61 (7): 28–35.

3

E-books in the School Library

SHONDA BRISCO

M any of today's school librarians would probably consider themselves technologically literate. In fact, many of them are early adopters of educational technologies, including Web 2.0 applications and software. Others not only adopt these new technologies but spend hours training other librarians and teachers to use these resources within the curriculum. As early adopters of new information technology, librarians are also cognizant of the need to provide their students with a wide variety of educational formats to make accessing and utilizing information easier. This includes providing resources that extend beyond the physical walls of the school library and outside regular school hours.

When it comes to providing the latest resources, school librarians have experimented with and used e-books in school libraries since the introduction of CD-ROM–based encyclopedias in the 1980s. Even today most middle and high school librarians provide some type of e-reference book for their students, whereas elementary school librarians are more likely to provide interactive reading programs through either CD-based programs or a combination of free online collections and subscription programs. According to an online survey of approximately 250 school librarians through the LM_NET discussion group, approximately 63 percent of high school librarians currently provide either free online e-book access or an online subscription of e-book content to their students, and 15 percent of both elementary and middle school librarians provide e-book content (Brisco 2009). Although some school librarians may still be reluctant to move forward in providing e-book content to their students, much of the concern seems to be based upon financial reasons rather than an unwillingness to embrace new technologies. In fact, with the recent publication of the American Association of School Librarians' *Standards for the 21st Century Learner,* most school librarians understand that the student's ability to access and utilize e-book content is a vital skill necessary for information literacy and future success in education. Unfortunately, those skills may be hindered by the school district's inability to provide access to the needed technological resources.

Despite the enthusiasm that is often linked to new technologies and the ability to access various e-book formats, school librarians may also be somewhat apprehensive in deciding how to go about selecting, managing, and maintaining the hardware and software needed to make these resources available to their students. Others may be waiting for a standardized format to be selected before they invest in these resources for their libraries.

Regardless of the exact reasons for the delay in providing accessibility of e-books in some school libraries, it is easy to see how overwhelming it could be to select e-books for students when the hardware, software, and applications are so varied. Within the past five years production and distribution of e-books within the school library market have exploded, making the selection of e-books and the technology needed to use them even more confusing for librarians who are unsure the expense can be justified within their continually shrinking budgets (McKenzie 2009). A study by the Association of American Publishers shows that sales of e-books in August 2008 were up 82.9 percent compared to August 2007 and up 53 percent for the year between 2007 and 2008 (McClure 2009). And yet, even with these trends, e-book purchases for school libraries have not been as brisk as those in public libraries.

Nevertheless, for those school librarians who understand the importance of making e-books available to students, providing the statistical evidence to show the value of these resources to administrators and educators, and how they might be integrated within the curriculum, is time consuming and even difficult for more isolated school librarians. Unfortunately, there are thousands of school librarians who take on double duty as the technology director as well as the school librarian on a daily basis; many others are being pulled in two or more directions by overseeing several library campuses throughout the week, with little time to evaluate each library collection thoroughly. Adding what seems to be yet another responsibility—justifying the purchase of e-books, in addition to training educators to use them—may seem impossible. Still, librarians who find themselves in this scenario may discover that e-books can provide even more content accessibility for more students and teachers than traditional print books.

For many, the packaging can often be the most uncomfortable aspect of e-books. Rather than a familiar, physical format, users access information online that seems an entirely different type of content than is traditionally used in the classroom. Regardless of the packaging, the concept of what makes a book *a book* has definitely changed. A book is no longer considered a tangible object with a hard cover wrapped around hundreds of pages filled with information. Today's book can be found in a wide variety of formats and can be accessed regardless of time or space. Much like the changes made in the physical formats of music within the past fifty years, resulting in an intangible product now accessed using different electronic methods, tomorrow's book may soon not physically exist. Instead, "the printed word will have evolved into electronic files that can be distributed, bought, sold, and consumed on digital devices" (Gomez 2008).

For many traditional educators, the lack of training in the use of new information technology and a misunderstanding of the difference between free, authoritative online content and peer-reviewed or scholarly subscription content and e-books only muddy the water when this new format reaches the classroom or school library. This confusion among even educated professionals can result in the inability of some school librarians to promote, advocate, or even teach students the access and use of e-book technology.

Despite the growing availability of e-books in public and academic libraries, studies have shown that many educators have not been exposed to e-books in their undergraduate training and most do not know how e-books could be used within the curriculum (Cavanaugh 2006). Yet, despite the lack of exposure, experience, or training, teachers are required to provide instruction in the use of this e-book technology to students for both research and recreational purposes (ISTE 2008).

According to the "Technology Counts 2008" report that determines how educators in the nation are utilizing and integrating technology into the curriculum, in 2009 the majority of states received a C grade for their work with teachers in preparing them for the effective utilization and integration of digital technology in the classroom. Although the level of training offered by these states was not as expected, it is important to note that many educators began seeking professional development courses on their own to learn some of the latest technological applications and how they could be used with their students (Orey et al. 2009).

Even as some educators move forward on their own to learn about the new technology, this trend is not consistent throughout the nation, resulting in many students and their teachers not being properly trained to access and use online resources or new digital technologies. In this case, the lack of training becomes a leadership issue that requires administrators to take complete ownership in educational technology. In other words, for teachers to become effective users of digital technology, district administrators need to invest on a continual basis in the appropriate professional training necessary for their educators (Goodstein 2007).

TYPES OF E-BOOKS FOR K–12 LIBRARIES

Despite the popularity of the latest Kindle, iPad, or hundreds of applications available for downloading, the majority of students in today's schools continue to access e-book content through desktop and laptop computers. Some of the most common e-book formats found in today's classrooms and school libraries include audio e-books, interactive e-books, and text-only e-books.

Audio e-books are digital versions of audiobooks that are available for downloading through the Internet. Generally, these require the student or teacher to download the e-book onto a desktop or laptop computer that utilizes a specific software program to allow the book to play, such as Windows Media Player. Some audio e-book programs allow users to download books onto their personal MP3 devices by creating an online account that keeps track of the downloaded items made available. Some of the most common providers of audio e-books for school libraries are NetLibrary, Books on Tape, OverDrive, Listening Library, and Recorded Books.

For early childhood, pre-K, and elementary levels, the interactivity of print, audio, and video creates an accessible product that provides not only entertainment but also reading scaffolding, encouragement, and support. Interactive e-books give emerging readers and struggling readers additional support without requiring continual adult assistance. Many of these products incorporate video formats of picture books coupled with read-aloud audio options (often available in two or more languages) as well as interactive links to access various applications such as online dictionaries to assist users in word recognition, pronunciation, and listening skills. Both stand-alone products and online access to e-book content are available through products such as BookFlix, Capstone Interactive, One More Story, Leapfrog, TumbleBooks, Kid Thing, and Big Universe.

Interactive and multimedia content is continually being added to enhance user interest and provide additional information, but the most common e-book content is text only. Generally these e-books are packaged as stand-alone products for downloading or accessing entirely online or are embedded within a larger database format that allows for several volumes of similar content (such as a reference title) to be made available and searched simultaneously. Some of the more familiar e-reference books available within periodical subscription databases are *Compton's Encyclopedia* and *Funk & Wagnall's New World Encyclopedia,* both available through EBSCO, and *U*X*L* reference titles, available through Gale.

For school libraries, some of the companies that provide subscription e-book content are Gale Cengage, Follett, EBSCO, ABC-CLIO, and Facts on File. Each of these companies has e-books that can be accessed from a laptop computer, but only a few, such as Follett, currently provide access of e-book content through handheld devices such as smartphones. Interestingly, even though trends in e-book access are moving toward access through handheld devices typically used by students, it is unlikely that many K–12 schools will allow this personal technology in the classroom unless the cultural acceptance of these tools changes. As educators and administrators struggle with ways to eliminate distractions in the classroom (cell phones, gaming devices, other handheld devices), digital communications technology is making these things a part of daily life for millions. Students continue to access, create, and share new content—including e-books—beyond the school walls. Within those walls, restrictions on the use of cell phones and other handheld devices continue to inhibit students from effectively utilizing some of the most common e-book resources, including those accessed from their local public libraries and even from their own home computers.

Anastasia Goodstein, author of *Totally Wired: What Teens and Tweens Are Really Doing Online* (2007), describes a typical day in the life of an imaginary teen, Judy Jetson. From the time she wakes up to her cell phone alarm to the time she walks onto the high school campus, Judy, like most teens, is engaged in either accessing or creating online content. Unfortunately, once these teens enter the school building, most electronic devices and online applications are turned off, filtered out, or locked down, placing twenty-first-century learners back into a nineteenth-century learning environment.

Fortunately, there are exceptions to this rule. Many teachers and librarians have advocated the right to utilize unconventional classroom technology, such as cell phones, to teach students how to use the online tools that allow for wireless access to e-book content. Rather than exclude these applications from the classroom, these educators are searching for ways to integrate many of the handheld devices used by teens into their curriculum. In her book *Toys to Tools: Connecting Student Cell Phones to Education,* Liz Kolb identifies several instructional components that can be added to the regular curriculum via cell phones. Among them are the classic e-books that are available for downloading to cell phones (Kolb 2008). Now, rather than having to purchase copies of a print classic, students can download the e-book to their cell phone and access the content digitally.

As these applications continue to grow, so do the possibilities for accessing and using e-books in the classroom. One of the latest for e-books is an iPhone application that allows users to download Amazon's Kindle software (known as Whisper) to the iPhone and iPod Touch, giving users a more modest version of the complete Kindle program. Another e-book software application for the iPhone—Iceberg Reader, created by ScrollMotion—allows users to download picture books and full-length young adult novels. The first e-book using the Iceberg Reader is the *Curious George Dictionary.* With more than six hundred illustrated entries as well as gaming options, this pocket-sized educational tool may eventually change the way students as young as kindergarten age access and use books (Teicher 2009).

As with most areas in education, funding often determines whether a program is implemented. Even though declining library budgets restrict the implementation of e-books in the curriculum, many school librarians have introduced their students and faculty to e-book content through the various free online collections. By introducing teachers and students to these resources and how they can be used, many school librarians are preparing their users for the ability to access subscription resource content and e-books when budgets allow them to become available; additionally, their students will be competent in using these tools when they get to college. Once students and faculty become familiar with these types of online resources, the transition to using e-books for research or recreational reading becomes easier.

The beauty of free online e-book collections is that they are easily accessible and require little or no additional software to access and use. Because most of these collections are made available through universities or philanthropic organizations that promote reading and literacy, most K–12 schools with Internet filters can access the sites without problems. Some of the most popular free online e-book collections specifically developed for use by elementary students include these:

Children's Books Online: www.childrensbooksonline.org
E-books for Young Readers: www.saskschools.ca/~ebooks/
International Children's Digital Library:
    http://en.childrenslibrary.org
Internet Public Library Kidspace: www.ipl.org/kidspace/
Storyline Online: www.storylineonline.net
Storyplace: www.storyplace.org

Some of the most commonly used free e-book collections available online for middle and high schools include these:

Bibliomania: www.bibliomania.com
Digital Book Index: http://digitalbookindex.com/about.htm
EText Center/Scholars' Lab: www2.lib.virginia.edu/etext
Google Books: http://books.google.com

Gutenberg Project: www.gutenberg.org
Internet Public Library: www.ipl.org/div/subject
Librivox: http://librivox.org
Manybooks.net: http://manybooks.net
Online Books Page: http://onlinebooks.library.upenn.edu/lists.html
Page by Page Books: www.pagebypagebooks.com
Read Print Library: www.readprint.com
World Public Library: http://worldlibrary.net/give-away.htm

Each of these e-book collections lets students examine various types of e-book content while offering the teacher and librarian opportunities to teach reading, research, and information literacy in new and creative ways.

CATALOGING E-BOOKS FOR K–12 SCHOOL LIBRARIES

Once e-book content is purchased for the school library, it may be difficult to quantify exactly what is owned. Unlike the tangible print book that takes up physical space on the library shelves, e-books provide content in a virtual environment that may not easily be noticed. As a result, unless the librarian is vigilant in showcasing e-book content through instruction or training, most students and teachers will not realize that this format is available.

One method to ensure that e-book content is found is by including the e-book MARC records in the library's online catalog. Just like searching for a physical book from the OPAC, users can also locate e-books available for access when the online catalog includes the e-book's MARC record. When search results are shown, both print and e-books are listed. In addition, by opening the e-book record, users can directly access the e-book content by clicking the hyperlinked access point located within the results record. This hyperlink immediately redirects the user to the actual e-book subject content located online or within the subscription database. Thus, you have a seamless entry point from the online catalog to the actual subject content without requiring the user to open new browsers or log in to new programs or databases.

Most database companies offer their e-book MARC records for down-loading from their website and provide customer support to help librarians install the records. Once the MARC records are uploaded to the library catalog, librarians can make changes to local content fields, if needed. Librarians interested in adding even more free e-book content found on the Internet by adding it to their online catalog and MARC records should consult Fritz (2007) or Weber (2002).

ACCESSING E-BOOKS IN K–12 SCHOOL LIBRARIES

Depending upon the type of e-books purchased, the decision about how to make these materials accessible must be made early in order to determine the cost involved and the specific technology that might be needed. Aside from determining the content needed, librarians must also evaluate the availability of the hardware and software necessary for accessing the electronic content. Unfortunately, this is generally the major disadvantage of e-books for many school librarians. Because e-book hardware such as laptops, notebooks, and handheld devices is so expensive, it often becomes cost prohibitive for school librarians to invest in the technology (Grant 2002). Popular e-book content may be easily downloaded for access by students through a personal iPod or smartphone, but the ability to purchase, as well as manage on a daily basis, several hundred of these devices and their software for students would be overwhelming for many libraries with limited staffing.

As a result, most school librarians purchase subscription access to e-book content that is housed within the vendor's website. Although this method can diminish the need for additional personnel to troubleshoot technological glitches on-site or from within the district, it may also restrict or eliminate accessibility to e-book content when the vendor's system is down, when customer complaints are not responded to quickly, or when issues of accessibility are not resolved. Weighing the different access options available requires, among other things, research into the availability of technological support within the school or the district.

Librarians should work closely with their district or campus information technology departments to determine the best methods for making e-book content available and discuss what types of hardware, software, and other applications can be brought to the classrooms and library. By sharing thoughts with your technology specialists about the specific types of content being considered, how it should be accessed, what responsibilities will be required of the information technology department for maintenance or support, and what additional hardware or software might be needed in the future, librarians can gain support for e-book use within the curriculum.

As e-book technology continues to change, librarians need to stay current on licensing issues, upgrades to software, and new hardware systems, for any of these may affect the library's e-book holdings. Terence Cavanaugh, author of several books and articles on the use of e-book technology in the classroom and library, provides an up-to-date list of e-book formats and software on his website, www.drscavanaugh.org.

MARKETING E-BOOKS IN K–12 SCHOOL LIBRARIES

Although some educators hesitate to add e-book content to their curriculum units or daily lesson plans, most students are quick to identify with and attempt to use new applications and apply them in new directions. For librarians who are often caught between these two groups, determining the best way to market e-books to their students while easing the fears of educators can be a challenge. Some methods for marketing e-books to students and teachers include

> Providing in-service programs for teachers and administrators, showing them how e-books are accessed and how they might be integrated into the curriculum.
>
> Showcasing e-books with parents during an open house event and giving parents home access passwords to encourage continual use of these resources by students after school.
>
> Offering to add e-book links to a teacher's online research module or classroom web page for ease in access by students.
>
> Including e-book information and access links to library newsletters or administrative e-mail to parents and teachers.
>
> Using audio e-books during booktalks with middle and high school students to show them how they can be

used while working out; traveling between home, school, and sporting events; or even relaxing.

Encouraging teachers at all levels to pair audio e-books with their print counterparts for transitional, struggling, or reluctant readers to allow for reading support outside the classroom.

Providing e-books in different languages to encourage ESL students to access reading materials from home for continual learning or to assist parents with homework or reading assignments.

Adding cover images of e-books with hyperlinks to the school library's web page, allowing immediate access to online resources for those who might not be aware of the materials.

Including e-book widgets (available from many e-book providers such as Gale Cengage, EBSCO, ABC-CLIO, Britannica, and others) to the school library's website, Facebook page, classroom web pages, and other websites.

Including icons of the e-books available along with the list of research databases, allowing users to locate available e-reference book titles easily.

Listing the titles of e-books available within the subscription databases (e.g., EBSCO provides several hundred full-text biographies and e-reference books within its subscription database collections) and creating hyperlinks to those sources on the library's website or within subject-specific research modules.

USE STATISTICS AND JUSTIFICATION OF COSTS

During the early years of e-book accessibility in public schools, the ability to determine use was not clearly defined. Some database companies that offered e-book content through their subscription databases provided administrative account access that allowed the school librarian to determine the monthly use of the e-book content through a log-in access password. However, within larger school districts this information may not have trickled down to the building or campus librarian. Instead, the information may have been sent to the district librarian, school administrator, or district technology director. Unless the school librarian knew who received this information or needed it for reports, many of them were not aware that this information was available to them.

As e-book vendors continue to modify their resources to make content more accessible to school librarians, it has become easier to obtain measures of e-book use through either direct administrative access or a monthly e-mail of use statistics from the e-book companies. Librarians can easily determine how to be notified of use statistics for their e-book content by accessing the e-book vendor's support web pages or by contacting the vendor to set up a monthly use report.

Despite the excitement of providing e-book content to students and teachers, librarians must continually justify the cost of e-books in relation to the cost of print materials. Although use statistics provide a great deal of information about which titles are most popular and how many titles are being accessed, the critical factors of the cost involved must be considered and justified during economically challenging years. The following quick facts can supply some of the justification:

> E-books provide 24/7 access of traditional print content
> and make it available to multiple simultaneous users
> regardless of their physical location.
> E-books have features such as hyperlinked information,
> read-aloud capabilities, dictionaries, and multiple
> language access instantly.
> E-book content is never lost, damaged, or overdue.
> E-book files can be downloaded, shared, or saved on
> handheld devices, flash drives, or notebook computers.
> E-books do not take up valuable shelf space in
> overcrowded libraries.
> E-books can be searched for and accessed from within
> the online catalog or the library's website through
> hyperlinks that direct the user to the content.
> E-books can be integrated into online bibliographies for
> special research projects and accessed immediately
> through digital pathfinders or research modules.

E-books can be accessed and shared by students
and parents from home at any time and used
to supplement instruction or homework
assignments.

E-books with multiple language options or speech
can be used by ESL students both in the classroom
and at home to encourage continual language
development.

E-books can be accessed during the summer months to
extend the availability of the school library's holdings
to students and their parents even when school is not in
session.

E-books can bring online content to students, teachers, and
parents in smaller communities without public libraries.

E-books can make accessing research content or reading
assignments easier for students who are homebound or
unable to attend school.

Students with reading disabilities such as visual impairments
can easily access online content and adjust the fonts or
utilize speech software to access reading or research
materials.

FUNDING RESOURCE OPTIONS

Regardless of whether e-books are considered justified or just a frill,
the ability to start and maintain an e-book collection requires funding
resources and solutions for sustainability. As librarians search for ways
to integrate new technology and twenty-first-century information literacy
skills into the curriculum and teach them to students, their instructional
goals may be limited by budgets that fluctuate with various economic
conditions, changes in educational policies, or even differing administrative ideologies. As a result, a reduction in funding for new technological
applications in the library may hinder many school libraries from providing
e-book content to their students.

Locating funding resources for the purchase of e-books requires that
school librarians be creative about how e-books will be used. Some ideas

for finding funding resources for purchasing e-books and equipment include the following:

> *Title I (Improving the Academic Achievement of the Disadvantaged) funds:* www.ed.gov/policy/elsec/leg/esea02/pg1.html
>
> *Grants available through various programs to increase literacy, such as the 21st Century Community Learning Centers grant:* www.learning.com/funding/21stcclc.htm
>
> *Target Early Childhood Reading Grants:* http://sites.target.com/site/en/company/page.jsp? contentId=WCMP04-031821
>
> *HP Technology for Teaching Grant Initiative:* www.hp.com/hpinfo/grants/us/programs/tech_teaching
>
> *EDS Technology Grant Program:* http://foundationcenter.org/sitemap.html
>
> *E-book publishers such as Sylvan-Dell:* www.sylvandellpublishing.com/ResourceGrant.htm
>
> *Other federal grants such as Title IID, Title III, and Gear Up grants:* www.learning.com/funding
>
> *Additional resources for school library grants are listed at Scholastic .com for Librarians:* www.scholastic.com/librarians/programs/ grants.htm

For more on grants available to school libraries, librarians may also consult print resources such as Anderson and Knop (2008).

ISSUES OF E-BOOKS IN K–12 SCHOOL LIBRARIES

As with any new resource within the school library, it takes some time for users to become familiar accessing the materials before they become effective users of the resource. Unfortunately, changes in digital resource accessibility, limitations in the access or use of various content, or the unexpected removal of e-content by the publisher can often make the library seem more restrictive to users who are accustomed to having access to a wide variety of similar content on the Internet. Yet, unlike the open Web, subscription services require libraries to protect proprietary content from unauthorized access and use. This results in requiring users to access this content through special library account numbers, passwords, or other methods that can prevent many students from taking full advantage of these unique digital resources.

Among some of the issues related to access to library subscription content is digital rights management (DRM). In short, "DRM is the technology that allows copyright owners to regulate and manage their content when it is disseminated in a digital format" (Houghton-Jan 2007). This can, in essence, restrict students from accessing specific types of digital resources if they do not own or have access to a particular type of hardware or software program. It also limits the way students can use this material for even educational purposes. For example, an audio e-book downloaded to a student's iPod in an MP4 format could not be transferred to a computer running only MP3 software. As a result, because the digital formats are incompatible, the audio e-book could not be used for a classroom presentation without modifying the original format. Unfortunately, in our collaborative 2.0 world, many students do not understand how e-book content is provided or the legal issues surrounding its distribution. As a result, many users of digital e-book and audiobook content look for open-source software programs that alter proprietary content so that it can be accessed, shared, and used without permission from the copyright owners.

Because subscription content that is used or shared without permission violates copyright law and breaks the contractual agreements made between the publisher, the vendor, and the school library/librarian, the issues surrounding DRM and the library's mission to provide information access by all users can be frustrating for both librarian and students. Copyright issues and plagiarism are continual problems in most high schools and universities, and it is important that school librarians discuss with students how the library provides e-book content, what guidelines are in place for the use of the e-book content, the students' responsibilities in using the content, and possible options for making digital content available to all users. In the meantime, school librarians must continue to stay current on DRM and what certain publishers provide their customers. Locating and supporting publishers that provide content free of DRM will help to drive new models of distribution to school libraries that make e-book content as easily accessible for use as printed materials.

Another problematic issue of e-books in school libraries is the inability of some students to access and use online resources from home. Although broadband connections have increased over the past decade and more rural and urban homes can get Internet access, the pricing structure offered to these individuals often prohibits high-speed access (Goodstein 2007). In many rural or outlying school districts, communication infrastructures that support Internet connectivity for online access to multimedia resources are still not in place. As a result, many students and even teachers have limited access to e-book content from both the Internet and their school's subscription services.

To best provide the resources needed by K–12 students, school librarians should not only survey their school population to determine what type of electronic access is available in the students' homes but also investigate the school community itself to determine the socioeconomic issues regarding online access, including the availability of online computers or other software needed to use the resources, the Internet access provided within the community (such as dial-up Internet access, T1 lines, or digital access), as well as the skills needed to access the school's e-book collection from off campus.

As e-books continue to make their way into school libraries and classrooms, librarians and teachers will discover that this instructional format, like others in the past, is merely another method for providing curriculum content to all learners. Just as television, DVDs, and even video games have transformed education and the way we think and learn, e-books will bring a new level of collaborative insight into our students' lives and help them engage in creative thinking while developing new ways to ensure educational success.

E-BOOK SUBSCRIPTION PROVIDERS FOR K–12 SCHOOL LIBRARIES

ABC-CLIO: http://ebooks.abc-clio.com
BookFlix: http://teacher.scholastic.com/products/bookflixfreetrial
Capstone Interactive: https://www.mycapstonelibrary.com/contact
　.html
EBSCO: www2.ebsco.com/en-us/ProductsServices/ebooks
Facts on File: http://factsonfile.infobasepublishing.com/Ebooks.asp

Follett: www.flr.follett.com/intro/ebooks.html
Gale Cengage: www.gale.cengage.com/servlet/GvrlMS?msg = k12
Marshall Cavendish: www.marshallcavendish.com
NetLibrary: http://company.netlibrary.com/aboutus.aspx
OverDrive: www.overdrive.com
Rosen: www.rosenebooks.com
Rourke Interactive e-Books: www.perma-bound.com/interactive-
  books/rourke.faces
TumbleBooks: www.tumblebooks.com

REFERENCES

Anderson, Cynthia, and Kathi Knop. 2008. *Write Grants, Get Money.* 2nd ed. Worthington, Ohio: Linworth.

———. 2006. *The Digital Reader: Using E-books in K-12 Education.* Eugene, Ore.: International Society for Technology in Education.

Brisco, Shonda. 2009. "E-books in the School Library Survey." Survey Monkey, http://www.surveymonkey.com/s.aspx?sm = xwlQkfWSm3w5Qr_2fcgiXwB Q_3d_3d/.

Cavanaugh, Terence W. 2006. *The Digital Reader: Using E-Books in K-12 Education.* Eugene, Ore.: International Society for Technology in Education.

Fritz, Deborah A. 2007. *Cataloging with AACR2 and MARC21 for Books, Electronic Resources, Sound Recordings, Videorecordings, and Serials.* 2nd ed. Chicago: American Library Association.

Gomez, Jeff. 2008. *Print Is Dead: Books in Our Digital Age.* New York: Macmillan.

Goodstein, Anastasia. 2007. *Totally Wired: What Teens and Tweens Are Really Doing Online.* New York: St. Martin's Griffin.

Grant, Steve. 2002. "Ebooks: Friend or Foe?" *Book Report* 21 (1): 50.

Houghton-Jan, Sarah. 2007. "Imagine No Restrictions." *School Library Journal* 53 (6): 52–54.

ISTE/International Society for Technology in Education. 2008. *The ISTE National Educational Technology Standards (NETS*T) and Performance Indicators for Teachers,* www.iste.org/Content/NavigationMenu/NETS/ ForTeachers/2008Standards/NETS_T_Standards_Final.pdf.

Kolb, Liz. 2008. *Toys to Tools: Connecting Student Cell Phones to Education.* Eugene, Ore.: International Society for Technology in Education.

McClure, Marji. 2009. "Turning a New Page in EBooks." *Information Today* 26 (4): 1, 18.

McKenzie, D. 2009. "Ebooks and 21st-Century Learning." *MultiMedia and Internet@Schools,* January 1: 27–28.

Orey, Michael, V. J. McClendon, and Robert Maribe Branch. 2009. *Educational Media and Technology Yearbook,* vol. 34. New York: Springer.

Teicher, Craig Morgan. 2009. "E-books Go Interactive." *Publishers Weekly,* August 24.

Weber, Mary Beth. 2002. *Cataloging Nonprint and Internet Resources.* New York: Neal-Schuman.

4

E-books in the Public Library

AMY PAWLOWSKI

I t is no surprise that thousands of libraries across the United States now offer access to e-books and downloadable audiobooks. In fact, it is almost expected that a library offer the service in one form or another. For e-books in public libraries, 2004 was a monumental year. Products had been peppering the market for a few years, but it was not until the offering of downloadable audiobooks that public libraries started showing a stronger interest in the service. In March 2004 a conference sponsored by the Open eBook Forum (now known as the International Digital Publishing Forum) titled "eBooks in the Public Library" was held in New York City. The conference brought together two hundred librarians, publishers, and vendors to discuss the pointed future of e-books in the public library space. The prediction made at the conference—"The e-book market in the public library space was 'set to explode'"—seems to have come to fruition (Rogers 2004). As part of the goal of providing information to the masses in a variety of forms, public libraries wisely helped set the pace of bringing e-books and downloadable audiobooks to their communities by first forming consortia to purchase collections—allowing them to keep the risk of the venture low while they tested the viability of such a service (Genco 2009). In 2009 well over eight thousand public libraries offered e-books and downloadable audiobooks. This statistic should be attributed to the popularity of the service seen by early adopters as well as by publishers' recognition of the advantages of offering public libraries a compelling selection of popular frontlist titles.

There are undoubtedly many benefits for public libraries to offering e-books and downloadable audiobooks. They raise circulation, offer a 24/7 service for patrons who may not have a schedule that allows them to visit the library, do not require shelf space, attract both "digital natives" and "digital immigrants," are cost effective since collections do not require replacements for damaged or lost materials, and allow lending flexibility (Genco 2009). Furthermore, purchasing an e-book does not include shipping, book processing, or other procedures that slow the delivery time. Although e-books and audiobooks are offered in a variety of different genres, public libraries tend to focus on the collection of popular materials. Because publishers are rather particular about the distribution and security of their titles, they do not offer their titles in e-book or downloadable audiobook format directly to libraries. Therefore, public libraries offering the service do so through a vendor who acts as a distributor for a variety of publishers and offers a service platform for discovery and delivery to a library's users and collection and statistical management tools for staff.

VENDORS AND PRODUCERS

A library may choose to offer popular trade e-books and audiobooks from more than one vendor, but titles are vendor specific and not cross-platform; if a library purchases a title from vendor A, it cannot make that title available in the collection and platform of vendor B. How the title is accessed (in-house or remote) and what users are able to do with it once accessed (e.g., read online, download, burn to CD) depends on the format offered by the vendor, the vendor's platform, and the digital rights management (DRM) from various publishers.

The list of producers and vendors that provide public libraries with e-book and downloadable audiobook platforms fluctuates, but currently there are three vendors that have a prominent presence in the market: OverDrive (a private company based in Cleveland, Ohio), NetLibrary (formerly a division of OCLC that was acquired by EBSCO Publishing in 2010), and Ingram Digital (an Ingram Book Company Content Group). Generally, vendors' platforms function the same, but there are differences in delivery methods, formats offered, publisher partnerships (titles offered), and the tool used for downloading audiobooks.

OverDrive broke into the library market by supplying public libraries with e-books patrons could download to desktops, laptops, and handheld devices (Reid 2003). The company worked with librarians to create a customized platform with many features, such as ILS (integrated library system) integration and a customized web-based catalog. The company eventually expanded its offerings to include downloadable audiobooks, music, and videos.

NetLibrary began offering titles that were mostly academic in nature. Public libraries picked up some titles, but there was not enough business. Eventually the company branched out by offering downloadable audio-books. It partnered with audiobook publishers, and libraries could offer their patrons both the vendor's academic books and popular audiobook titles. The popularity of downloadable media, specifically audiobooks, sparked Ingram Book Company to enter the market in early 2009. Building off the platform frameworks create by OverDrive and NetLibrary, Ingram's platform (MyiLibrary Audio) offers downloadable audiobooks and the same functionalities as its competitors.

OverDrive, NetLibrary, and Ingram Digital partner with thousands of publishers (including major publishers such as Books on Tape, HarperCollins, Penguin Group [USA], and Harlequin) to offer a wide selection of titles rang-ing from frontlist to self-help to romance.

Baker and Taylor is another vendor that has shown strong interest in the market. At the 2010 Consumer Electronics Show, the company unveiled Blio, new e-book reader software. The announcement that accompanied the unveiling claimed that the "software will launch with an online store featuring more than 1.2 million titles—from best-sellers to travel guides" (Griggs 2010). Because of Baker and Taylor's strong presence in the library market, one could draw the conclusion that a library-friendly version of Blio could soon follow.

Public libraries also collect reference e-books. Treated much like a database, reference e-books in large and medium-sized public librar-ies are rather common. The Gale Virtual Reference Library, ABC-CLIO/ Greenwood's Digital Collections, Credo Reference, Sage Reference Online, and Oxford Reference Online are commonly seen products. They offer users access without the need of a reader; printing, downloading, and e-mailing features; unlimited simultaneous use; and 24/7 access to remote users. They provide libraries an opportunity to extend the reference collection space without using crowded shelves and offer greater discoverability of content through the online full-text format.

Since hitting the market, all vendor platforms have progressed in functionality, features, and offerings. The range of compatibility has also increased over the past few years because of new formats offered and the implementation of new technologies. Factors such as the accessibility of titles on a variety of different devices, titles offered, and customizable features seem to sway libraries to work with one vendor over another. In addition, there are many small features or benefits that may influence a library's preference. These may include the actual process for downloading an audiobook title or how a vendor responds to a library's suggestion for improving the service. OverDrive seems to have won the confidence of both public libraries and publishers. Its ascendancy in the market is attributed to publisher confidence in the security of content, high-quality customer service, and flexibility of delivery tools (Genco 2009).

FORMATS

Initially, e-books were available only in OEB (Open eBook) and PDF formats, and audiobooks offered as downloadable titles were available only in WMA (Windows Media Audio) format. Today, public libraries offering e-books for checkout and download do so in four different formats: EPUB, Adobe PDF, OEB, and Mobipocket (also known as Mobi or PRC). Digital audiobooks are available in both WMA and MP3 file formats.

The EPUB e-book format is considered the new e-book industry standard. Short for "electronic publication," the EPUB standard was developed by the International Digital Publishing Forum (IDPF), the trade and standards association for the digital publishing industry that consists of retailers, e-book manufacturers, software developers, and publishers. It is XHTML content wrapped in a ZIP file package (.epub) that contains XML files to describe the content and metadata (Mironchuk 2009). It features a small file size, reflowable text, and e-reader optimization and supports embedded content, allowing, for example, a Flash video to be embedded within an e-book. EPUB-formatted titles are compatible with the Sony Reader as well as with Windows and Mac computers using Adobe Digital Editions.

Before the adaptation of the EPUB format, most publishers offered their e-book titles in OEB or Adobe PDF format. Superseded by the EPUB format, OEB is a legacy e-book format based on XML. This format was used by many publishers between 1997 and 2007 and is still supported. An Adobe PDF e-book is a PDF file that is DRM-protected using Adobe DRM. It is, more or less, a static document or screen capture of the publication; the text cannot be resized to fit within a user's computer or e-reader screen. However, one of the main strengths of the PDF format is its ability to preserve the layout of complex documents, such as encyclopedias and reference titles. Because most public libraries started to develop their e-book collections in the early to mid-2000s, PDF and OEB formats can still be found in current collections.

EPUB, Adobe PDF, and OEB titles are all DRM-protected and are managed and read using Adobe Digital Editions software. In addition, this

DEVICES	FORMAT			
	Audiobooks		E-books	
	MP3 audiobooks	WMA audiobooks	PDF	OEB
PC	X	X	X	X
Mac			X	X
MP3 players supporting DRM-protected WMA files	X	X		
Other MP3 players	X			
iPods	X			
Sony Reader			X	X
nook eReader			X	X

TABLE 4.1 *NetLibrary Compatibility Chart*

software enables users to transfer titles to other computers and allows the transfer of EPUB and PDF titles to Sony Reader devices. As a reader, Adobe Digital Editions allows users multiple options for viewing, reading, and annotating their materials.

The Mobipocket format, which has a .prc file extension, enables users to read Mobipocket titles on Windows-based computers as well as on smartphones and most PDAs (e.g., BlackBerrys, Windows Mobile, and Palm devices). The free Mobipocket Reader software is required and must be downloaded to any computer or handheld device for reading or transfer. Each installation of Mobipocket Reader includes a personal identifier, or PID number, that uniquely identifies a copy of the reader. Users who have access to Mobipocket titles must associate every PID number with their account from their library's digital platform. Mobipocket titles offered via a library's downloadable collection are text based, DRM-protected, and rather small in size (around 200–600 kB). The format offers features such as customizable display, resizable text, built-in full-text search, and the ability to annotate and highlight. Currently, OverDrive is the only vendor offering the format.

Devices	Format Audiobooks*
PC	X
Mac	X
MP3 players	X
WMA devices	Limited
iPods	X
iPhones	X

TABLE 4.2 *MyiLibrary Audio Compatibility Chart*

*Ingram Media Manager converts the audiobook into the appropriate format for the device.

Downloadable audiobooks are available in both WMA and MP3 formats. WMA audiobooks, the more popular of the two formats, are built using the Microsoft Windows Media Audio format. Thus, compatibility is mostly limited to Windows-based systems and devices, although newer versions of the OverDrive platform allow some WMA files to be transferred to iPod devices. Audiobooks are also offered in the more common sound file format, MP3, which is interoperable with any MP3 player and iPod devices. In fact, many publishers are apprehensive about releasing materials in MP3 format because of the inability to control use and distribution.

Not all vendors offer all formats, and some may offer other types of downloadable media in addition to e-books and audiobooks. Also, the compatibility of formats depends on the computer, device, and vendor delivery tool. To date, NetLibrary offers e-books in PDF and OEB formats, with newer content more heavily weighted in PDF, and audiobooks (which the company refers to as eAudio books) in WMA and MP3 format (see table 4.1). Ingram Media Manager converts the audiobook into the appropriate format for the device, whether it be PC, Mac, MP3 player, or iPhone (see table 4.2).

OverDrive offers the most format options for libraries. E-books are available in three formats (PDF, Mobipocket, EPUB), and audiobooks are available in two different formats (MP3, WMA). Music files are available in WMA format and video files in WMV format. New content offered by publishers via OverDrive tends to lean toward the EPUB format (see table 4.3). The company has also hit the mobile market with applications that search a library's collection, check out, and download a title all from the device.

DELIVERY METHODS

E-books and audiobooks in public libraries are delivered through a vendor platform that generally includes a web-based catalog of materials (used for discovery) that works in tandem with proprietary software (such as Adobe Digital Editions) to deliver and display, or play, the title. Generally most platforms allow libraries to customize lending periods and the number of titles a patron is able to check out at any given time. The look, architecture, and functionality of the platforms vary by vendor.

With some vendors, a library directs its patrons to the vendor's website. The library's collection is then visible to patrons once an account is created using their library card or a returning patron has logged in. A library's collection site may consist of e-books, audiobooks, and e-journals, depending on what the library has subscribed to or purchased from the vendor. E-book titles are made available to patrons to open and view right from the collection's website using an online reader. Libraries can also offer

DEVICES	FORMAT						
	Audiobooks		E-books			Music	Video
	MP3	WMA	PDF	Mobipocket	ePUB	WMA music	WMV videos
PC	X	X	X	X	X	X	X
Mac	X		X		X		
MP3 players supporting DRM-protected WMA and WMV files	X	X				X	X
Other MP3 players	X						
iPods using the Mac OMC console	X						
iPods using the Windows OMC	X	X				X	
Sony Reader			X		X		
nook eReader			X		X		
Mobile Device Apps							
Android	X				X		
BlackBerry	X						
iPhone	X		*		*		
Windows Mobile	X	X				X	X

TABLE 4.3 *Overdrive Compatibility Chart*

* In development

PDF titles as a downloadable format by purchasing an Adobe Content Server license (NetLibrary 2009).

Vendors' audiobooks can be offered as downloadable titles directly from the collection's website. When a download is initiated, users access titles one of two ways. One is by saving the file directly to the computer and using a media player to listen to and transfer the title to a portable device. A second option, if available, is to use the vendor's free software application for searching, managing, downloading, and listening to a library's downloadable audiobook collection. The application may also function as an audio player, offering play speed, volume control, and resume-listening features. In addition, once a title is checked out and down-loaded to the patron's computer, the software assists with transfers to sup-ported devices. Once the software is installed on their computer, patrons can also search the library's collection from their own homes or offices.

Another way vendors offer materials to libraries is through a web-based catalog that is designed specifically to match the library's established web presence and includes a custom URL. All formats the library purchases for its collection appear in the catalog, whether book, audiobook, music, or video titles. The catalog is open for anyone to browse and functions much like an online shopping site, wherein a patron selects titles to down-load and then enters a library card number (which is checked against the library's ILS) to check out and enable the download process. A vendor that offers many different levels of digital rights (such as burn to CD and trans-fer to a variety of formats) lists the rights or what a patron can or cannot do with a title once it is downloaded. For example, with some vendors, Adobe Digital Editions software allows users to view and manage e-books in both PDF and EPUB formats. In addition, the software can allow users to transfer PDF and EPUB titles to other computers and e-reader devices.

Vendors offer applications that act as the manager, player, and facili-tator for downloading, transferring, and burning audiobooks, music, and videos from a library's collection. These applications can notify users when a title has expired, allow users to organize their downloaded materials, and allow users to delete materials from their computers once they are done with the title or the title has expired. As a player, the application can offer a variety of playback and title navigation options such as multiple play speeds, bookmarking, and a resume button. Some applications also facilitate users' transferring of a checked-out title from their computer to a portable listening device and the burning of allowed titles to CD.

Some vendor platforms do not require a patron to select the correct format of a downloaded title. Instead, the application pulls the title down and requires patrons to select the type of device (Windows Mobile, iPod, or MP3) to which they wish to transfer the title. Applications can also detect whether there is enough space on the player for the transfer and offer up a screen from which users can select which part(s) of the title to transfer.

To ensure more visibility of their collection, public libraries typically purchase MARC records enhanced for e-book and downloadable audiobook holdings. The records are added to a library's OPAC, and through the 856 field each record links directly to the title on the appropriate vendor's website. The MARC records also contain information about special features and denote the formats available for that specific title. NetLibrary, OverDrive, and MyiLibrary Audio all offer MARC records.

LICENSING AND LENDING MODELS

All e-books and WMA audiobooks are protected by DRM files, which, aside from deterring unauthorized access and duplication of copyrighted files, are used to set the parameters of how a patron may use the file. These parameters may include the length of time a title is accessible once checked out or how a title can be downloaded or printed. More recently, vendors have started to offer the DRM-free MP3 format from cooperating publishers. Because these files do not have DRM-like protection, vendors are relying on patron agreements to exercise control over the content. For example, prior to checking out an MP3 title in the OverDrive platform, patrons are required to accept the "Terms of Use for MP3 Titles," which states that they will not share or copy the file and will destroy the file once the loan period is over.

Vendors typically offer two licensing model options for their materials. Items can be added as single-purchase titles or as part of a subscription. Single-purchase titles function much like physical materials. After a title is purchased, a copy is added to the collection, and when a user checks out the title it is removed from circulation. If a title is currently checked out to a patron, a user may place a hold on the item. Libraries may choose to purchase additional copies of high-circulating titles to alleviate long hold lists. Many reference titles can be purchased individually as well, but access is generally set for unlimited simultaneous users, which comes with a higher price tag per item. Pricing is usually based on a public library's population served.

Subscriptions offer extended accessibility of titles because holds are never necessary. Once the title is selected and the annual subscription price paid, libraries have unlimited access to the content. However, only a few publishers offer subscriptions through vendors. Larger publishers shy away from this model because it is not as cost effective for them as the single-purchase approach. In effect, because public libraries tend to prefer popular frontlist titles, collections typically consist of single-purchase titles because trade publishers sell title by title. There are reference platforms available as subscription products as well. Again, access is set for unlimited simultaneous users, and pricing is based on the population served. Some reference publishers, such as Credo Reference, allow libraries to subscribe to 100 or 250 titles in its collection and, each year, select and deselect titles based on their needs.

More often than not, libraries tend to have the same lending period for their physical materials as they do for their digital collections. For example, if a library's print books have a lending period of twenty-one days, they set the lending period of their e-books to twenty-one days as well. If a library has a shorter lending period for books on CD (e.g., fourteen days), they usually make the lending period for downloadable audiobooks the same. A nice feature that alleviates long hold lists is customized lending periods. Offered by OverDrive and MyiLibrary, customized lending periods allow a library to define a set of predetermined loan periods from which a patron can choose upon checkout.

To figure out the best formula for the circulation of digital titles, a library must consider many variables, and this may take some trial and error. In theory, much like a popular print or books-on-CD collection, a good digital collection always has a decent number of materials available for checkout. Along with adding new titles on a regular basis, this can be accomplished by properly determining the appropriate maximum number of titles a patron can check out, the lending periods associated with each format, and how many duplicate titles a library is willing to purchase. The Dayton Metro Library's formula is to purchase two or three copies of a best seller to start. Each month, the library checks the holds on items and purchases additional copies to meet a ratio of four holds for every one copy. In difficult budget times, however, the ratio may increase to five to one (Jean Gaffney, personal communication, 2009).

COLLECTION MANAGEMENT TOOLS

Since vendors also act as distributors for publishers, the tools for collection management are considered part of a vendor's platform. Like proprietary player software, collection management tools are vendor specific. Hence, if a library offers two different platforms, titles for each collection must be added via the appropriate vendor's collection management tool. The tools offered by vendors are rather efficient and offer many different options for adding items to a collection. In general, collection management tools are web based, include tools to make the financial transactions easy, and can add purchased titles to a collection within minutes of a completed order.

Libraries can order titles from vendors by searching the available materials catalog, or they can choose from vendors' prepackaged title lists prepared by a collection development team. Vendors may also offer supplemental collection development tools that automatically add new titles directly to the collection on a quarterly basis. In addition to online tools, vendors offer personal assistance through collection development teams who tailor custom orders or collections based on the library's set requirements.

OverDrive also offers supplemental collection development tools such as download standing order plans and a "Holds Manager." Download standing order plans function like a standard print standing order plan: a library chooses which publishers and a desired number of upcoming e-book or audiobook titles they would like to add automatically. OverDrive's Holds Manager helps manage patron waiting lists. A library can set a holds ratio, maximum price range, and maximum number of titles, and the Holds Manager automatically adds new copies of titles to the collection when the waiting list reaches the parameters set.

STATISTICAL TOOLS AND LIBRARY USE

Vendors are aware of the importance of providing solid statistics for digital collections, and they offer robust report tools to aid the analysis of collection holdings and circulation. These tools are a terrific resource for promotion and customization as well. Features of these tools vary by vendor but generally include reports for overall use or individual title use. Format, date range, subject or genre, and individual library (if multiple libraries or branches are sharing the collection) are examples of facet types in the reports themselves.

Vendors' reporting tools can offer detailed collection development and usage reports and allow libraries to organize their collections, manage account preferences, and establish security levels for users. Reporting tools can also offer flexible reports for title and user statistics. Often reports can be exported to Excel, making it possible to combine data sets so libraries can look at their collections in even greater detail.

The use of e-book/audiobook platforms in public libraries is seeing noteworthy success. A 2009 survey developed by Barbara A. Genco, library consultant, and Michael Santangelo, electronic resources manager for Brooklyn (New York) Public Library, reports that 88 percent of responding libraries have seen an increase in library circulation of these materials. The highest reported growth was 1,200 percent by Hennepin County Public Library in Minnesota, with the bulk of responses ranging from 31 percent to 300 percent growth (Genco 2009).

The CLEVNET eMedia Collection is an example of a platform that has judiciously built a solid collection and whose statistics reflect the benefits. The service, offered to libraries participating in the CLEVNET consortium (a group of thirty-one libraries across northern Ohio, including the Cleveland Public Library), opened in April 2003. Since the beginning of 2004 there has been a growth of 1,000 percent in cardholders using the service. The collection has also grown to meet this demand. In July 2009 it held just over 31,000 copies, dwarfing the collection's total of 3,700 copies in December 2004. Even with what is considered a medium to large collection, the titles are not just sitting on the digital shelf. On average, 42 percent of the collection circulates every month. According to OverDrive CEO Steve Potash (personal communication, August 2009), the success

The River Forest Public Library Experience with the Kindle

BLAISE DIERKS

The River Forest Public Library serves the 12,000 residents of River Forest, Illinois, a suburban community near Chicago. The library began circulating the Amazon Kindle in July 2008 after three first-generation Kindles were donated. Once the library staff had the opportunity to explore the devices, the next step was getting them to the patrons, but there were several challenges. To purchase and download content, the Kindle was linked to the library's Amazon account, but the Kindles could not circulate with the ability to purchase content to be charged to the library. Several questions had to be answered: What content should be loaded? How should the device be cataloged? What type of case should it circulate in? What should the lending rules and fines entail? Additionally, Amazon's terms of service made the legality of lending the device ambiguous. Despite all of these questions and issues, the library proceeded.

The adult services, technical services, and circulation departments at River Forest worked together to answer these questions and get the Kindles circulating. The questions of content and circulation went hand in hand. The library decided that each Kindle would circulate with preselected themed content. The first three themes were popular fiction, popular nonfiction, and mystery and suspense, for which $180 was spent on the initial content download. Once the Kindles were loaded, they were deregistered from the library's Amazon account, allowing the patron to read content currently on the device without downloading new content. Staff worried about selecting the deregister option the first time around; who knew what would happen? Fortunately, all content remained on the device, and it was possible to reconnect it to the library account later. This fixed-content solution was the easiest for River Forest at the time, but certainly it is not the only solution. Another option is to download content each time, thus taking advantage of Amazon's wireless delivery of content. River Forest chose the fixed-content option because of the need to deregister and reregister otherwise.

River Forest cataloged each Kindle as a single item attached to one bibliographic record, and titles on the devices were not cataloged. This was a reflection of how the library initially saw the lending of the Kindles. It was less about the content on the device and more about the actual device. Staff felt that patrons just wanted to try one out. Other libraries that circulate e-book devices catalog them differently and may include titles on separate bibliographic records. This would be a valuable way of providing patrons the choice and control over what they can read on the Kindle.

Certainly one question that has plagued libraries is the legality of lending Kindles. Although Amazon's ambiguous terms of service and inconsistent responses to inquiries on the lending of Kindles did not clarify the matter, River Forest decided to move forward and began lending the Kindles without contacting Amazon first. Should the library be told to stop lending them, it will.

News of the Kindles spread fast, and holds began to pile up quickly, particularly during the holiday season when patrons wanted the "try it before you buy it" option. After circulating the Kindles for nearly a year, the library added two second-generation Kindles to the circulating collection and an in-house Kindle for use in the library without waiting for holds. Holds have consistently been high, even with five devices in circulation. On average there are ten holds per device, with a total of fifty to seventy patrons waiting for all five Kindles. Holds cannot be placed on the in-house Kindle. The Kindles are circulated to patrons for three weeks at a time with no renewals. They are not sent out through interlibrary loan or used in place of traditional print interlibrary loan for patron requests.

The Kindles have held up well during circulation. They are housed in a zippered bag with a leather case and a charger. Minor problems with the devices were resolved, including the inability to turn the device on or off and deleting all content. Amazon provided troubleshooting assistance in both situations. Luckily, once a device is reregistered, the content previously purchased can be downloaded to the device again. Overall, the Kindles have been surprisingly durable during circulation.

No formal evaluation has been done to obtain patron feedback, but comments provided by patrons returning the devices have largely been positive. They are impressed that the library already has e-book readers and happy to have the opportunity to use one without buying it first. Moreover, patrons feel the Kindle is easy to use and handy for commuting. Conversely, patrons do want to download their own content and dislike some of the Kindle screen features.

Overall, the Kindle lending project at River Forest Public Library has been very positive. The staff learned from the experiment and will continue to develop the program on the basis of their experience and that of other public libraries. Moving forward, River Forest will reevaluate its Kindle lending policies and investigate the lending of other e-book reading devices in order to be innovative in providing devices and content for its patrons. ■

the CLEVNET eMedia Collection has seen is characteristic of a library that keeps the collection fresh and markets the service appropriately.

Initially, when e-book/audiobook platforms appeared in the public library space, libraries were not quite sure where the collection fit within their circulation reports. Most were not counting downloads because they were treating the collection like a database as opposed to a material type. The same rings true today, with usage statistics reported in a variety of ways. A majority of libraries include electronic content usage statistics in reports, followed by those that include a discrete downloadable materials report. Interestingly, some libraries are including the circulation numbers within the media and print circulation statistics (Genco 2009).

An example of how pioneering libraries are reporting statistics comes from the New York Public Library, which considers the collection its "virtual branch" and counts all of the collection's statistics within circulation reports. The collection, eNYPL, circulated over 500,000 titles between August 2008 and July 2009, which ranked higher in circulation than some of their branch libraries (Miriam Tuliao, personal communication, 2009).

WORKFLOW LOGISTICS

Because different people use and enjoy books in a variety of different ways, e-books and downloadable audiobooks are usually considered (as a whole) an additional material format, much like a book on CD is to a print title in a collection. Reflecting this trend, public libraries have a tendency to leave the shaping of the collection to their collection development department. In addition, since most platforms focus on popular materials, development of the collection is treated much like the popular print collection. The technical aspects of the service are most often managed by the library's web services manager or librarian, who typically manages any technical issues with the vendor and takes care of patron support. Should a library participate in the loaning of reading devices such as the Kindle, Sony Reader, or nook, the management of the service may fall to multiple departments within the library. This process is discussed in detail in the Kindle case study at the River Forest Public Library.

At the Denver Public Library, the collection is managed by the senior special collection librarian, Joan Hansen, who spends about four hours a week working on the collection and submitting orders for new titles almost every week. The collection, which offers e-books, audiobooks, and videos, has a monthly target budget amount to keep the collection fresh. Working from suggested title lists, the collection development librarian adds titles that best fit the reading tastes of patrons using the collection. The web services librarian attends to the collection's patron support questions. According to Janet Ryan, web services information librarian at the Denver Public Library, support questions do greatly fluctuate, but on average the library answers three to four questions a day. Because Denver's site is an OverDrive customized platform, changes to the site, either in the site's appearance or how the collection is presented (e.g., highlighting popular subject groups or formats), are also the responsibility of the web services librarian. Most often, the librarian responsible for site changes works with the vendor to implement any changes or enhancements.

Budgeting for an e-book/audiobook collection varies from library to library and depends on the size of the institution, the size of the budget, and how many libraries share the collection. According to the Genco/ Santangelo 2009 survey, only half of all libraries that responded reallocated funds from physical material formats to purchase electronic downloadable copies. The survey also reported an even split between how downloadable content was represented in a library's materials budget. The two most common practices were to allocate funds out of a separate line for all downloadable materials and to include the budget within the electronic resources line.

MARKETING

Public libraries that currently offer a digital collection have found that drawing awareness to the collection takes a variety of efforts. Vendors are also aware that libraries need help getting the word out about the service. As a result, they may have a department that is solely dedicated to helping libraries market the vendor's service. The vendor's department may offer custom print materials (e.g., bookmarks, posters, brochures), web collateral, media outreach assistance, custom training, in-library customizable display materials, ad slicks, sample press releases, and web banners and graphics.

Internal marketing and training are two important factors for generating successful use of an e-book/audiobook collection. Since the service functions as an at-home product, library staff do not have regular contact with or are not required to use the service on a regular basis. Miriam Tuliao, assistant director of central collection development at the New York Public Library, points out that NYPL's biggest challenge is the independence and remoteness of the service. Because of this, the staff are not as engaged in the same way as they are with materials that reside in the physical library. Although the circulation of the eNYPL collection is strong, the library is trying to think outside the box when devising ways to engage staff as well as patrons who are not aware of the service.

Offering training or orientation sessions for staff and patrons is an effective method for helping potential new users learn about vendor services (Peters 2007). Training and orientation sessions also give users an opportunity to experience the service and ask questions in person as opposed to the normal method of troubleshooting by e-mail or phone. According to Janet Ryan, the Denver Public Library offers training classes for its patrons as part of its promotional and outreach efforts. Organized by the web services librarian, the classes are held in the library's computer lab and usually have more participants than the lab can hold.

Another factor in marketing e-books is the library catalog. If MARC records are in the library catalog, the discovery of the titles is more likely, says Jean Gaffney, collection development manager at the Dayton Metro Library. The library's collection sees 50 percent of its e-book use generated from searches in the online catalog.

CONCLUSIONS

Undoubtedly, the most important factors for library success with digital platforms are the availability of popular frontlist titles and the accessibility of the service. The popularity seen thus far is rooted in the efforts of libraries to configure good formulas, promote the collection, and keep their collection fresh by regularly adding new materials. Because they have figured out (most likely through trial and error) good formulas for their services, libraries can certainly learn best practices from one another, but they should keep in mind that one library's equation for a well-used collection may not work for the next library. A good formula is one that works best for the organization and its service population. It may include many different factors including how frequently titles are added, what types of titles are added, what loan periods are determined, and what types of marketing (both internal and external) are used. Because the market is still fairly new and changes and enhancements are still emerging at a quick rate, libraries should also remember to evaluate their formulas regularly to ensure they are getting as much use out of the collection as possible.

The past few years have brought many significant improvements to e-book/audiobook services, but there is still room for growth. Some vendor tools offered for e-book and audiobook downloads have glitches and could be improved upon, and libraries that offer different vendor platforms often find that the different vendor-specific access procedures confuse patrons. There is also no doubt that, as the service and offerings grow, the different processes for acquiring digital materials will do the same and may become too complicated for patrons (especially "digital immigrants") to understand. And there is still the question of how a library will be able to offer purchased e-books and audiobooks if a vendor's platform should become unavailable.

The fact still remains that libraries are seeing e-books and downloadable audiobooks succeed as a service, and librarians are optimistic for what the future holds. One item on their wish list is deeper integration with ILS catalogs. The Baltimore County Public Library currently has a platform with both OverDrive and MyiLibrary, making it difficult to explain the different processes and availability of materials to patrons. Enabling deeper integration, such as integrating a tool that would display the availability of the title within a library's ILS catalog and indicate checked-out digital materials within a patron's record, would seem to be a logical next step. Library staff members would also like to see the service become less complicated and more accessible via handheld devices.

Future plans for vendors involve fixes and enhancements to current platforms. With EBSCO Publishing's purchase of NetLibrary in early 2010, EBSCO's plans are to enhance the NetLibrary platform by incorporating e-books into EBSCOhost, its e-content platform, creating an integrated e-book, database, and e-journal service (EBSCO 2010). OverDrive's CEO, Steve Potash, is focusing the company's goals toward usability improvements, which involves more intelligent applications that streamline (reduce steps) the approach to the checkout and download process while incorporating navigational help. In addition, the company has already released mobile applications for the BlackBerry, Android, Windows Mobile, and iPhone and plans to offer improved mobile tools in conjunction with the expanding market. Over the past five to six years, public libraries have seen e-books and other downloadable materials well received by both their communities and librarians. This new environment, paired with lower costs and better offerings from publishers, should assist with the further growth and popularity of the service.

REFERENCES

EBSCO. 2010. "EBSCO Publishing to Acquire NetLibrary Division from OCLC." EBSCO Publishing news release, March 17, www.ebscohost.com/uploads/thisTopic-dbTopic-1418.pdf.

Genco, Barbara A. 2009. "It's Been Geometric! Documenting the Growth and Acceptance of eBooks in America's Urban Public Libraries." Paper presented at the World Library and Information Congress, 75th IFLA General Conference and Council, August 23–27, Milan, Italy.

Griggs, Brandon. 2010. "Bold New E-readers Grab Attention at CES." CNN, January 8, www.cnn.com/2010/TECH/01/08/ces.ereader/.

Mironchuk, Ivan. 2009. "What Is ePub?" DCPI, September 30, www.databasepublish.com/blog/what-epub.

NetLibrary. 2009. Patron Driven Acquisitions. NetLibrary, http://library.netlibrary.com/PatronDrivenAcquisition.aspx?ekmensel=18_submenu_38_link_5.

Peters, Thomas A. 2007. "Implementing and Sustaining a Digital Audiobook Service." *Library Technology Reports* 43 (1): 30–34.

Reid, Calvin. 2003. "OverDrive Inks Library, Yahoo! E-book Deals." *Publishers Weekly* 25 (2): 15.

Rogers, Michael. 2004. "OeBF-Sponsored Gathering Tackles Content, Delivery, Usage, Economics, and the Dire Need for Standards." *Library Journal* 129 (7):23.

5

The Academic Library E-book

LINDSEY SCHELL

E-books are an ever-increasing staple in academic libraries, where 24/7 desktop delivery of content has become a standard user expectation. Early e-books became available to academic libraries around 1999, from NetLibrary and Project Gutenberg. NetLibrary contracts held by the University of Texas at Austin and others signaled a bold step into the burgeoning information age and kicked off a decade of digital growth that included e-books, e-journals, OpenURL technology, expanded wireless access, and social media. Indeed, ten years ago e-books were viewed as a passing fad with little attention paid by the general readership and mostly negative mention in the media. As of Bowker's 2008 annual statistics, e-books were a $67 million segment of the publishing industry; now, more publishers are offering content each year, and significant research and development money is being poured into competing portable e-book reading devices (R. R. Bowker 2008).

THE E-BOOK LANDSCAPE

Today, e-books are sold in a wide variety of formats, genres, interfaces, and pricing models, as is seen in table 5.1. Types of e-books now available include popular reading, scholarly monographs, monographic series, reference works, downloadable audiobooks, collections based upon scholarly bibliographies such as EEBO (Early English Books Online), and free classic texts that are out of copyright such as those in Project Gutenberg.

E-book vendors include third-party aggregators such as NetLibrary, E-book Library Corporation (EBL), ebrary, Safari, Humanities E-book, Gale, and MyiLibrary as well as a variety of individual publishers such as Springer, Elsevier, Cambridge University Press, Duke University Press, Palgrave, and Wiley-Blackwell. Some third-party aggregators, such as Gale, offer both in-house publications and titles from partner publishers; others, such as Elsevier, offer their titles through direct contracts or through aggregators like EBL. The transferability of digital content, and in particular e-books, makes them extremely agile products to package and repackage as the market dictates.

Pricing models also vary from publisher to publisher. Early e-book models were based on the traditional title-by-title selection by librarians, similar to contemporary practices with print books. This model is still used by some vendors today; designated librarians can select from an online title list—updated each month by the vendor—after which an invoice is generated and MARC records for the selected titles are delivered electronically for downloading into a local OPAC. The MARC records provide OpenURL links to the e-book content.

The next pricing model to hit the e-book market was subject-based subscription packages. These packages typically contain anywhere from 100 to 1,500 titles based on broad common subject areas such as business, computer science, or health science and provide a mix of new and standard titles in that field. Some packages add new titles each year while retaining the backlisted titles while other packages swap out older titles in favor of new or revised content. These subject-based packages are paid on annual subscriptions to accommodate the addition of new material each year.

The newest pricing model to hit the market is pay-per-view, or what some call patron-driven purchasing. The point of this model is to provide patrons with a wide variety and volume of content while charging them only for materials they actually use. In these models, MARC records are

	Title by title	Subject packages	Pay-per-view	Single-user check outs	Simultaneous users	MARC records	Download files
NetLibrary	X		X	X		X	
ebrary	X	X			X	X	
EBL	X		X		X	X	X
Safari		X			X		X
MyiLibrary	X	X			X	X	
Gale	X				X	X	X
Humanities E-book		X			X	X	

TABLE 5.1 *E-book Vendor Features*

loaded into a local OPAC, and when a library patron opens the content, a charge is generated on the library's invoice. The parameters for these charges vary greatly and must be carefully negotiated to contain costs up front. Indeed, one of the biggest concerns librarians have with adopting this model is the fear of runaway costs generated by users indiscriminately opening the e-books. Careful planning during the implementation stage can avert this kind of worst-case scenario. Negotiable points include:

- Which MARC records are downloaded into the local OPAC. Limiters by list price and publisher are optional.
- The number of times a book can be rented (viewed) before it is purchased.
- The cost per rental.
- The cost for purchase.
- How long a book can be viewed before a rental charge is generated, with some vendors offering a five-minute grace period to eliminate accidental charges.

- Whether a human mediator is required to approve an e-book transaction, such as a librarian approving a user-selected purchase of e-books over $100.
- How many times a book can be viewed after purchase.

Some vendors solidify these parameters at the start of an annual contract; others allow libraries to adjust the parameters as needed throughout the contract period. This kind of flexibility allows libraries to control costs instantaneously and make adjustments during unpredictable budget years. Pay-per-view options are currently offered by NetLibrary, EBL, Elsevier, and Wiley-Blackwell as well as some foreign-language vendors such as Chinamaxx and Eastview; ebrary's pay-per-view program is in development.

In addition to the various pricing models, vendors offer different access models. The checkout model is based on the traditional print library where one book can be used by one patron at a time and multiple copies of the same e-book can be purchased to accommodate high demand. The checkout model for access is commonly associated with title-by-title purchase models. The unlimited-access model allows multiple users to open the same title simultaneously and is more commonly used alongside a package or pay-per-view purchase model.

Finally, e-books are delivered in a variety of formats, the most common being HTML, which can be read through a standard Internet browser, or PDF, which can be accessed through Adobe Acrobat or a vendor's proprietary interface. Some such interfaces require a user to download additional software, drivers, or plug-ins—something to consider before contracting with an e-book vendor, since these technical requirements may impact the setup of library computer workstations or require additional instruction for patrons using e-books on personal laptops. Access to e-books, both in the library and remotely, is also affected by issues such as whether the vendor offers IP address recognition or individual user log-in/passwords. Another consideration is whether the vendor offers OpenURL linking that can be run through local link resolvers such as SFX (ExLibris), 360 Link (Serials Solutions), or WebBridge (Innovative Interfaces). The presence of OpenURL linking significantly increases the discoverability of e-books, not only through the library's OPAC but also through licensed databases, Google Scholar, and other web-based research tools.

THE UNIVERSITY OF TEXAS EXPERIENCE

The University of Texas at Austin has taken a highly experimental approach to collecting e-books over the past decade and now offers access to over 600,000 e-books. Its first e-book contract, with NetLibrary in 1999, provided access to five hundred titles. Soon the experiment grew to include both title-by-title and subject package contracts with companies such as ebrary, Safari, and IT Knowledge. Later it added disciplinary databases with e-book content such as EEBO (Early English Books Online), ECCO (Eighteenth Century Collections Online), Sabin Americana, Early American Imprints, and many others. In 2007 it began a pay-per-view pilot with EBL, and today it continues to look for ways to integrate e-book purchasing into its larger collection building by adjusting print approval plans and budgets to work in concert with the e-book endeavors. The university has been fortunate to participate in several consortial arrangements for e-books. Although it has never formally marketed e-books, it has incorporated them into undergraduate information literacy curricula, instructed faculty in incorporating e-books into course management software (Blackboard is used on the UT Austin campus), and featured e-book products on the library website's spotlight section.

Another unique feature of the university's e-book program is its involvement with the Google Books project. The Google Books project made its public debut with five partner libraries in 2004, with a goal of digitizing the contents of the world's best libraries for public use. Those libraries, Oxford University, Harvard University, University of Michigan, Stanford University, and the New York Public Library, were originally estimated to contribute fifteen million volumes to the project. UT Austin joined the project as a partner library in 2007, committing up to one million unique works from the Benson Latin American Collection to the massive digitization project. The motivation for joining as a partner library was to improve the discovery of these unique works and support public domain access.

The partnership is ongoing and the results have been quite successful. The top-viewed title contributed by UT receives approximately 3,500 hits per week. The Google Books project is undoubtedly the largest digitization project ever undertaken and has created quite a stir in both the publishing and library worlds. Everything from the project's standards for digitization and metadata to Google's approach to copyright law has encountered close scrutiny. Only time will tell the outcome of the legal challenges Google faces over the project and the global impact of the sea change Google has imposed on the publishing and library industries.

FUNDING E-BOOK PROGRAMS

The funding of an e-book collection from existing library budgets is no small consideration. Careful planning and negotiation with the selected vendor or vendors is required to make sure library users get access to the most content for the library's money. Perhaps the first step in planning an e-book budget is to identify subject/genre areas that will support the success of the program. By looking at existing user patterns, librarians can target areas of content users are already seeking online. Many libraries have noticed a decline in use of print reference materials, with most patrons preferring the convenience and speed of online answers. In this case, offering a selection of reference e-books, either selected title by title or in a package such as Oxford Reference Online, Sage Reference Online, or Credo Reference, is one way to supplement the authoritative content library patrons require in an online format.

Another target area might be classic literature for English classes, where assignments may focus on close reading. E-books in this area offer a convenient way to perform keyword and proximity searches for textual analysis. Yet another common pattern is the desire of those in the sciences to access the latest publications in the field, perhaps using single chapters from several new volumes but rarely needing books published more than three years earlier. In this case, a subject-based e-book package with annually updated titles could best suit these users. Once the target audiences, subjects, and format needs are identified, the library can search for a customized e-book plan to best suit its needs.

The next step is to determine whether the new e-book content will replace print purchases or duplicate them. If the library cannot afford to duplicate content, then it is likely to reallocate the funds previously used for print content in the target area to the new e-book plan. If duplication is desired, the funds used for print can be cut in half, with half redirected toward e-books, or funds from another area can be used to supplement the new e-book plan. Of course, funds can also be diverted from subject areas identified as no longer needed or receiving too little usage. A reasonable starting target for e-book expenditures is 10 percent of a library's total collection budget, working up to 25 percent as users demand it.

In addition to identifying target areas for e-book success, libraries can modify existing approval plans to help fund e-book initiatives. For example, many e-book aggregators offer titles from publishers that are duplicated on print approval plans. Thus, the library may elect to block certain publishers on the approval plan in favor of online access through the chosen e-book provider. Because some patrons prefer print over e-books, provisions can be made to allow the supplemental title-by-title purchase of print books when a patron specifically requests it in lieu of an e-book. One challenge to be considered if you rely upon an e-book provider in lieu of receiving print for certain subjects or publishers is that the e-book edition of a title is often released on a six-month delay. Publishers cite this release strategy as a way to retain print sales in an ever-declining market. However, the strategy poses serious concerns for libraries wishing to provide up-to-the-minute content to users, particularly those who are well aware that the content is available, if only in print.

In e-book budget planning, usage statistics can be the most useful tool for determining target areas of low and high priority. Such statistical data can be pulled from the print approval plan and the acquisitions and circulation modules of the ILS on publishers, prices, subject areas, and quantities. After analysis, certain publishers may stand out as high cost and low use, perfect candidates for a user-driven e-book plan rather than automatic purchase through a print approval plan.

PURCHASING AND PROCESSING WORKFLOWS

E-books can create the need to alter purchasing and processing workflows within the academic library, for they are a unique product with qualities similar to both print books and online journals. Thus, the requirements for managing e-books are a hybrid of these two more familiar worlds. E-book vendors are sometimes the same publishers with whom the library already has established relationships, like Gale, ProQuest, or Springer, but they can also be relative newcomers like EBL. As discussed above, there are many options for purchasing, and thus for the invoicing of e-books—from one time purchases of individual titles or packages, to annual subscriptions of new titles in subject-based packages, to quarterly invoicing of pay-per-view e-books. The myriad options become confusing to traditional acquisitions and cataloging units set up on the monograph/serial binary workflow. Add in the question of who is responsible for cataloging the titles and establishing online linking through the OPAC or link resolver, and assume the library will be purchasing e-books from more than one vendor—the scenario quickly becomes a tangled web. A few basic adjustments prior to purchasing e-books can alleviate some of the confusion:

- Establish separate and unique fund codes for e-book purchases. This allows for easy tracking of expenditures by vendor and package.
- Designate one person to coordinate e-book purchasing. Depending on your current setup, it may make the most sense to assign this task to the person already handling online databases and e-journals, since the contract and licensing elements of e-books are similar.
- If necessary, coordinate with subject specialists before purchasing e-books to eliminate overlap between print and online purchases.
- Make sure existing acquisitions systems allow for the tracking of purchases and the ability to gather usage data. The e-book vendor may offer an administrative module to assist with this task.
- Ask for EDI invoicing. EDI (electronic data interchange) is available from nearly all e-book vendors to ease payment processing and eliminate paper waste.

Most academic libraries, and state-funded libraries in particular, are required to undergo periodic audits. Therefore, it is essential to be able to answer the questions "Did we get what we paid for?" and "What, exactly, do we own?" as they relate to online resources. Differing requirements for detail in this area dictate the kinds of data the library will want to retain, how long to retain it, and who is responsible for retaining the information.

LIBRARIAN BUY-IN

Creating buy-in for an e-book program is critical to establish before the contract is signed. One of the biggest attitudinal challenges to implementing an e-books plan may not come from patrons but rather from library staff. Librarians in particular may object to the acquisition of e-books for a variety of reasons, including the reallocation of funds away from traditional print collections, the perceived lack of librarian control over titles in e-book packages or pay-per-view plans, the lack of tangible items in exchange for money spent, the seeming dereliction of a library's archival duty, the anecdotal "evidence" that patrons do not like or want to use e-books, and the supposed withdrawal of trust in the librarian's or subject specialist's selection expertise.

One strategy to create staff buy-in is to share the aforementioned statistics regarding circulation, publishers, cost, and subjects. It is difficult to oppose a rational cost/benefit analysis of low-circulating materials. Additionally, a frank discussion about the evolving role of the library as a just-in-time collection rather than a just-in-case collection can be helpful in developing support for e-books. A rational presentation of the cost of purchasing and maintaining a print collection versus the cost of purchasing and maintaining an e-book collection can assist in building buy-in. Finally, make sure staff understand that, although acquiring e-books requires the reallocation of some funds, it does not have to be an all (print) or nothing proposition.

SHARING E-BOOKS ACROSS LIBRARY CONSORTIA

Sharing e-books through consortial arrangements can be a highly cost-effective way to introduce them to a collection. Since the management of the contract and invoicing are typically handled by the lead facility in the consortium, the burden of training local staff with new skill sets is reduced. Often the downloading of MARC records to the OPAC is handled centrally as well, further relieving consortium members of added work. In addition to the obvious benefits of competitive pricing through consortia, group selection of title-by-title e-books can create a diverse and rich collection. UT Austin participates in both the University of Texas

System consortium (fifteen campuses), purchasing NetLibrary e-books through a title-by-title program, and the state-funded TexShare program, which acquires NetLibrary e-book packages. With the University of Texas System plan, over forty librarians make monthly title selections, which are reviewed by the director of research services at the Austin campus before a final decision and purchase. This arrangement guarantees an e-book collection built collaboratively and with the needs of all members taken into consideration. The TexShare program includes the acquisition priorities of participating academic, public, and school libraries, so the collection includes many fiction, mystery, romance, do-it-yourself instruction, and other nonfiction titles that would not typically be purchased through UT's print approval plan but receive high usage from the academic population. In both consortial arrangements, duplication of titles can occur but is not viewed as problematic, since the NetLibrary contracts include a single-user model and duplicate copies allow for broader access.

Another example of consortial e-book purchasing is the OhioLINK consortium. OhioLINK purchases e-book collections directly from publishers. Collections usually contain all frontlist titles for the given year and include reference and monographic titles. But rather than link to publisher platforms for access, OhioLINK purchases the content to host locally on its own servers and interface. OhioLINK's interface is the OhioLINK Ebook Center, or EBC, which is run on open-source software. Maintaining an e-book platform requires a considerable amount of technical support but has many advantages, including cross-searching of all publisher content, customizing interface features and help screens for the local user group, eliminating annual access fees to multiple platforms, guaranteeing perpetual access, and selecting the metadata to include in the searchable index.

MARKETING E-BOOKS TO FACULTY AND STUDENTS

Marketing e-books can be as formal or informal as needed, depending on the culture of the library. Most library vendors offer on-site training and webinars that can be customized to the needs of local library users. Links to e-books can be embedded within course management software such as Blackboard and Desire2Learn or linked from online course reserves. Posters and bookmarks can often be obtained from e-book vendors. Some libraries add an "e" sticker to the spine labels of corresponding print editions of e-books or place tear-off e-book advertisements with URLs and database names alongside the print. The library website can be used to promote e-books through homepage search widgets, features, and spotlights as well as in the electronic resources section of the website. Perhaps the most effective way to promote the use of e-books is to incorporate them into the library's information literacy initiatives, discussing them alongside print books as another valuable tool in one's research repertoire. If e-books are new to a library's offerings, they can be marketed as a pilot or beta test. Subsequent usage statistics can be generated to justify further purchases.

Discovery and access are key to informal marketing tactics, so OpenURL linking should be maximized in addition to loading MARC records and cover images into the library OPAC.

CHALLENGES AND ISSUES

There are, of course, challenges that accompany the purchase and use of e-books in the academic library, some of which have relatively easy solutions and some that are part of the ongoing discourse in scholarly communication and digital information. Below are some of the more common issues that arise with the use of e-books.

Patrons who still want print. Inevitably, some patrons will complain about the library's purchase of a title in electronic format when a print copy is not also available. It is natural for people unfamiliar with e-books to be uninterested in learning to use them and even to demand a print "replacement." These patrons can be offered one-on-one instruction in using e-books, or the library may decide to maintain a small fund for the purchase of print copies of titles otherwise available only in online format. At UT Austin we have such a fund and a policy to purchase any print title requested by a patron. This policy is consistent with our overall customer service philosophy, and we have found that, although the number of these requests is very low, the goodwill generated with our patrons is quite high.

Digital rights management (DRM). Vendors apply various technologies to prevent unauthorized access and duplication of copyrighted multimedia files (Hawthorne Direct 2009). Every e-book vendor employs a different version of DRM with its products, and it is incumbent upon the library to investigate this portion of the contract and its implications for e-book accessibility before licensing.

ADA compliance. Many universities are required to comply with Section 508 of the Americans with Disabilities Act. The provisions of this law extend to the accessibility of web-based research tools provided by the library. ADA compliance varies across e-book interfaces, and vendors may not be willing to upgrade their products at the libraries' request. Therefore, it is imperative that library staff investigate the accessibility of an e-book interface prior to licensing. Most universities have an office on campus that can assist with the assessment by offering screen-reading software and accessibility consultations.

Portable devices. Libraries may wish to offer portable e-book reading devices such as Amazon's Kindle, Sony Reader, or the nook. Keep in mind that these devices may require proprietary software to display e-books or require e-books sold by a single vendor in a proprietary format to operate properly. Not all e-book vendors allow downloading of their content to such devices, nor can all devices utilize such downloads. Additionally, portable e-book devices are expensive and difficult to repair should they break, all issues to take into consideration when calculating the cost of an e-book plan. For a detailed study of one such device, see "The Penn State University Sony E-book Reader Project" in this chapter. The majority of e-book vendors currently in the academic library market offer e-books intended to be read on computers with Internet connections. Of course, the ongoing development of devices such as G3 network phones and MP3 players (for audiobooks) continues to push the boundaries of possibility with regard to e-book content provision.

Licensing. Most e-book products require a license, and the library should ensure that the license contains language that allows for the maximum benefit to library users. The top concerns include:

- Is someone on the library staff trained in license negotiation and educated about local license parameters?

- What content is included and how can it be accessed and used?
- Who are the accepted users?
- How does the vendor assure online performance, technical service provision, and archival preservation/perpetual access?
- What is the mechanism to handle disputes?
- Are e-reserves and course packs allowable?
- Are usage statistics guaranteed in the license and are they compliant?
- Does the vendor allow interlibrary loan?
- Are there access provisions for people who are visually impaired?
- Are traditional fair-use provisions explicitly ensured by the license, or are there restrictions?
- Are print and download options available, and if so, how much of the content is included?

A recent alternative to the traditional license is SERU (Shared E-Resource Understanding; see NISO 2008). SERU, approved by NISO and now being adopted by many vendors, allows libraries and vendors to come to agreement on basic contractual obligations without the exorbitant overhead of a formal license negotiation.

Printing. One of the longest-running challenges with regard to e-books is printing. Publishers have long tried to protect their content copyright through the restriction of printing in e-book interfaces. Vendors often claim they are caught in the middle between protective publishers and the desire to improve customer experience with the product. Adding to the frustration is the lack of uniformity with regard to e-book printing allowances. Some vendors allow printing up to a certain percentage of the total text while others limit printing to a specific number of consecutive pages. All such limits are an imposition to library patrons who may wish to print a whole chapter or undetermined number of pages from various sections of an e-book. The great debate over printing is ongoing and something that should be discussed with vendors during contract negotiation.

The Penn State University Sony E-book Reader Project

ANNE BEHLER

P rompted by the emerging popularity of electronic reading devices and the continued migration of academic content from paper to electronic format, the Penn State University Libraries partnered with Sony Electronics during the 2008/9 academic year to study the utility of electronic readers and e-books in the higher education environment. In conjunction with the project, Sony donated one hundred model PRS-505 Readers to the University Libraries, which we used in several different test scenarios. The overall goals of the Sony Reader Project were to investigate the utility of portable e-books in a research library collection; the effect of reading devices on teaching, learning, and reading; the utility of such a reading device for individuals needing adaptive technologies; and how our licensed and locally created digital content could be repurposed for use on portable reading devices.

To carry out this investigation, the Sony Readers were deployed in several scenarios: in library lending, in both first-year Honors English and first-year Library Studies seminars, and in the Library Services to Persons with Disabilities office.

The University Libraries supported the project by coordinating all content acquisitions, loading, and cataloging, a process that required logistical ingenuity. Because the Sony Reader is a consumer market product, the Sony licensing and DRM models were not ideal for the academic setting. Content purchased through the Sony e-book store requires creation of a title library on a personal computer. Each of these libraries can be used for up to five Sony Readers, with a USB connection between the devices and the computer as the vehicle for loading the content onto the devices. In addition, only one library can exist per computer, because the device-to-computer link is based on hardware-to-hardware recognition. To accommodate the hardware limitations this model presents, the project team used VMware software on two dedicated computers for the project. This software allows for the creation of several virtual machine profiles on a single computer. For the purposes of supporting the one hundred Sony Readers, the team created twenty virtual machines, half on each of the two dedicated computers. A spreadsheet was created to track the accounts associated with each machine, and as

Sony store content was purchased for the lending scenario, both the readers and the content were cataloged. Specific titles were noted in the contents field of the catalog record, so that the readers were discoverable by device or by their content. Library users who checked out the readers were invited to participate in an online feedback survey.

In the classroom setting students were issued readers preloaded with the content for the course. Students were also instructed on the process for loading their own content onto the readers, an endeavor that sometimes required the assistance of free software called Callibre, which can be used to reflow many different content formats, including PDFs and RSS feeds, into the proprietary Sony Reader file format or into an optimized PDF form for better viewing on the devices. The students shared feedback on their experiences through periodic surveys and video interviews, and the students in the Honors English classes gave end-of-semester presentations to a representative from Sony Electronics and members of the Penn State faculty at the close of the fall 2008 semester.

Readers were issued to library users with disabilities with the hopes that there was some application for individuals with sight impairment or dexterity limitations. Unfortunately, these individuals did not find the Sony Readers easily navigable; the buttons and text size were too small, and the process for navigating from one title to another was not easily recalled by memory.

Feedback received from participants in all scenarios revealed that, in general, users admired the sleekness of the Sony Reader and were enthusiastic about the portability it offers. Users found the E Ink grayscale technology to be easy on the eyes, and many users appreciated that the Sony Reader is a unifunction device that does not distract them from the process of reading.

On the other hand, users were not shy about expressing their criticisms of the devices. The PRS-505 had major issues with battery life and ease of charging, which have been addressed in later iterations of the Sony devices. In addition to battery trouble, users noted a slow refresh time when turning pages and a general lack of interactive features such as annotation and highlighting capabilities. Although many people noted that they enjoyed the single purpose of the device, equally as many expressed a preference to read texts on a multifunction device that supports web browsing, computing, and so forth. Other salient findings were in relation to students' habits while using the devices. Although the e-book readers are promoted as mobile devices, 92 percent of students polled reported using them only in their dorm rooms. They were not specifically asked why, but the project team guessed that this might be due to their need to be near note-taking tools, such as their computers, while reading. Students were also asked whether they focused strictly on reading while using the PRS-505s, and their responses overwhelmingly illustrated that they continued to multitask while reading.

From a library perspective, the DRM on the Sony e-book content was a handicapping issue. Because of the extremely complicated VMware logistics, only one person was authorized and able to load content onto the readers, making something like an on-demand service for patron borrowing of titles impossible. Beyond the specific experience with the Sony Readers, it is essential for the library to turn its focus to content more generally. Although users had a wide variety of opinions about whether the readers were useful, or would be in the future, all participants expressed the idea that it is important for them to be able to use content any way they need or want to. This is going to be the driving force behind what the Penn State University Libraries do in taking this project forward. The project team plans to continue working with vendors and publishers to provide feedback on their products with an eye to what our users need and a focus on issues of accessibility and portability of e-content. ∎

Interlibrary loan. The purchase of print books automatically conveys the right to lend those books through ILL services. This right is not, however, automatically implied with the purchase of e-books; access to e-books is typically governed by a license that restricts use to registered library users (current faculty, staff, and students). The right to provide access to e-books through ILL services is yet another area that must be investigated and negotiated prior to contracting with an e-book vendor. Publishers are hesitant to allow ILL for e-books because of the loss of control once the e-book has been distributed beyond the initial purchaser. Fearing the kinds of content vulnerability experienced by the music industry with the advent of MP3 file sharing, publishers are keen to control copyright and cost recovery on e-books and have largely failed to take advantage of distribution breakthroughs made possible by current technology. Such breakthroughs include the ability to distribute individual pages or chapters of electronic content and the ability to link to content and increase visibility through OpenURL linking. Costs associated with traditional print-based ILL are the cost and speed of delivery as well as the return condition of the book. All of these concerns are made obsolete by e-books, and the funds budgeted by libraries for traditional modes of delivery could be redirected toward publisher lending fees if an appropriate model were offered. Pay-per-view models may be one viable option for allowing libraries to share content beyond their licensed primary user group.

MARC records and loads. MARC records may or may not be automatically included with an e-book contract, and they may be available for an additional fee. Some vendors do not provide "full" records but instead offer an abbreviated form of MARC records that includes bibliographic information but not LC subject headings, tables of contents, or notes. As is the case of some pay-per-view e-book vendors, these brief records are available for rental books, and full records are provided after purchase of specific titles. In such arrangements, electronic batch loads of records for purchased titles are delivered on a periodic schedule and locally loaded into the library's OPAC, replacing the associated brief records. Locally established load profiles can be created to automate this process more efficiently, and the records can be delivered along with an EDI invoice.

Discovery. Discovery, in the modern library context, refers to a variety of strategies employed to enhance the user's ability to locate resources through improved search interfaces, metadata, resource linking, and access. Traditional discovery methods for print collections revolved around the library's catalog, in which librarians created access points (author, title, subject) that directed users to appropriate parts of the text, since the text itself was not accessible. Book indexes, concordances, and journal abstracting services provided further discoverability in the print-only world. In contrast, with an e-book the full text itself is accessible. Entire new areas of research are possible because the text is immediately accessible and not hidden behind confusing or incorrect pointers. Future discovery tools should allow a user to search across all texts in a platform-agnostic manner and drill down seamlessly to specific parts of a text. This could be delivered through a combination of pay-per-view, open source, licensed content, local digital copies, and even print, without having to navigate the current confusing library bureaucracy.

Plagiarism. As digital content becomes more prevalent, so too increase the opportunities for plagiarism. Wholesale copying of text is easier with e-books in HTML than it is for those in PDF format, though newer versions of Adobe Acrobat are capable of copy-and-paste functionality. Although there is little libraries can do from a technological angle to prevent plagiarism, it is nevertheless important to inform faculty of this heightened possibility and to offer anti-plagiarism strategies to interested library users.

Textbooks. Academic library users are increasingly interested in obtaining course-assigned textbooks in e-book format. Some vendors offer packages of textbooks to universities, and the distribution and financial management of such packages are sometimes placed under library oversight. These online textbooks can be delivered through compatible course management systems or selected/purchased by students on a title-by-title basis and downloaded to compatible portable reading devices. Current challenges with e-textbooks include determining whether the library is the most appropriate campus entity to manage the textbook contract and, if so, how to address the payment, access, and distribution of textbooks for the entire student body. The price structures for these contracts are still very much in development, making contract negotiation difficult in a market with few opportunities for comparison shopping or established best practices.

CONCLUSION

E-books constitute a fast-growing segment of the publishing industry and a rising percentage in library collections budgets. Library users have demonstrated their voracious appetite for e-books through high usage statistics and sales figures for portable reading devices. The market offers a wide range of products, price models, and titles to suit virtually any library collection and budget. After a decade of growth in the e-book market, some publishers are still slow to offer their content in electronic format or offer e-books only with highly restrictive DRM limitations. Additionally, print and electronic editions of books are not always released simultaneously, creating a challenge for libraries to offer the latest content in the timeliest fashion without duplicating purchases. Despite these challenges, e-books are sufficiently entrenched in the desires of library users, and the market will only grow as interfaces, pricing models, and reading devices continue to improve.

REFERENCES

Hawthorne Direct. 2009. "Digital Rights Management." Hawthorne Videoactive Report Glossary of New Media, www.videoactivereport.com/glossary/2/letterd.

NISO. 2008. "Shared Electronic Resource Understanding." National Information Standards Organization, www.niso.org/workrooms/seru.

R. R. Bowker. 2008. *Bowker Annual of Library and Book Trade Information.* New York: R. R. Bowker.

6

Acquiring E-books

CAROLYN MORRIS AND LISA SIBERT

E books are an exciting addition to the world
of electronic resources and to the world of
books. Libraries and providers are eager to incorporate e-books as fully as
possible into the mainstream of materials available to libraries and to users.
Whether seen through the lens of existing print material processes or existing electronic resources processes, e-books have presented new and unique
challenges and opportunities in terms of collection development options,
acquisition and cataloging processes, and access. Recognizing that libraries
and e-book providers are working together to update existing and define
new processes, in this chapter we suggest efficient and effective methods
for acquiring e-books. We cover a variety of topics for acquiring e-books,
including the types of e-books available; potential points of concern, such
as updates and ongoing fees; information about the business models under
which e-book providers are operating as well as the methods and routes
by which libraries can acquire e-books; various access models available
and the potential pros and cons of each; best practices for workflows
and processes throughout the life cycle of an e-book and specifically for

licensing e-book content; and key points for cataloging e-books and using an electronic resource management system to manage e-book collections.

E-BOOK TYPES

> As e-books move further away from conveying a story or content in the way print-based books do, we may well ask at what point is an e-book really no longer a book but something else? . . . Our traditional concept of content consumption is changing because of technology, which will ultimately have a profound impact on the concept of a book as new generations of readers mature and gravitate to new technologies. (Nelson 2008, 44)

As in the traditional print book market, there are several different types of e-books currently being published. In general, the forms that an e-book can take are familiar: reference, textbook, monographs in series, and the more traditional or standard monograph. Where e-books diverge from their print counterparts, however, is in the distinction between these forms. The lines between the types of e-books are more blurred than with print books, which can be either attractive or troublesome. Furthermore, the lines are blurred between e-books that appear to be monographs and those that more closely mimic other electronic material such as e-serials and databases.

E-reference

We think of reference books as being those books to which we turn to find information that is factual in nature: dictionaries, encyclopedias, and thesauri; books of acronyms and abbreviations; biographies, directories, guidebooks, and handbooks; maps, atlases, and almanacs; bibliographies; and books of quotations and statistics. Updated versions of these materials may be periodically published and released; updates usually include new information and are produced in a systematic, predictable manner. With the availability of reference e-books (or e-reference), however, updates can be produced much more quickly than with print and can either be integrated into the existing text or appear as separate volumes, editions, or releases of the e-book. If updates are periodically performed to the existing text rather than in the form of a new edition or volume, the e-reference can start to look more like a database than a book; if updates are released regularly as new volumes, the e-reference can start to look more like a serial than a monograph; if, however, the publisher releases updates in the form of new editions, the e-reference retains the look and feel of a traditional print reference book. When considering an e-reference acquisition, the library should ask the publisher or provider if updates are integrated or released separately, how often updates are produced, and whether the updates are included in the price paid or require payment of additional fees.

E-textbooks

E-textbook acquisition raises some of the same questions as e-reference acquisition. Textbooks are analogous to reference works in that if updates are necessary, these are usually handled in a scheduled manner. Due to the nature of e-books, e-textbooks can be updated as needed, either in the form of supplementary material or as direct updates to the e-textbook as it appears on-screen. Whether it is the library or a student who is considering an e-textbook, it is important to discern up front how the publisher handles these updates, whether notifications are sent, and how fees for updates are calculated, much like the circumstances described above for e-reference.

E-literature

The form of e-book with which most people are most familiar is that of the traditional electronic monograph, or individual title—published once and not meant to be subject to updates in content. As with their print coun-terparts, these can be further subdivided by audience, such as scholarly or academic, children's, or popular; by fiction or nonfiction; or by any number of other categorizing schema such as genre, subject, or discipline, determined by the publisher or provider. E-books that have received the most attention in 2008 and 2009 have been the individual titles—these are the e-books that have made the Amazon Kindle and other e-book devices like the Sony Reader and nook successful in bringing e-books to the mass marketplace.

E-monographs-in-series

Like its print cousin, an e-monograph-in-series is distinguishable by its separate parts, which usually take the form of volumes released throughout the year, or more or less frequently, depending on the publication schedule. The e-monograph-in-series feels like the print monograph-in-series in that the release schedule is systematic and scheduled, the series has an overarching theme or common thread, and each part can stand on its own as a separate monograph. When pursuing acquisition of an e-monograph-in-series, it is important for the library to determine the release schedule, the number of parts scheduled for release, and how costs are calculated for each part, for the series, or both. It is also important to consider how and whether the e-book provider will notify the library when new parts are released, and how and whether those parts appear as discrete items on the e-book platform (or viewer or reader). If the parts are not distinguishable from one another, the e-monograph-in-series starts to take on the appearance of a database rather than a monograph. It is important to consider this in the decision to acquire an e-monograph-in-series set, for it affects the ease with which the user is able to access the content contained within the parts.

BUSINESS MODELS

In an increasingly competitive global marketplace, new technologies and economic realities are forcing book publishers and wholesalers to make significant changes to their business models. The move toward digitization has wide-ranging implications for publishing organizations, impacting everything from their strategies to their corporate structures. The unbundling of content from the physical book provides new opportunities for distribution and creates new value propositions for authors, publishers, and end users (Tian and Martin 2009, 74).

In this environment, e-book vendors and publishers have endeavored to find purchasing models that appeal to libraries yet protect content from piracy and still generate or at least protect revenue. As a result, there are a variety of options available to libraries wishing to create e-book collections. A definitive "best practice" business model has yet to emerge for either libraries or publishers. In 2008, e-book revenues accounted for only 2.9 percent of the total U.S. book market. Only Taylor and Francis reported double-digit e-book revenue figures, with e-books accounting for 10 percent of its revenue in 2008 (Worlock 2009, 9). It is likely that models for e-book delivery will continue to evolve as the market matures.

Subscription

Subscription packages generally allow libraries to buy access to a large number of e-books for a set period of time. Frequently, subscription packages consist of backlist titles that publishers make available to aggregators knowing the print book sales have already run their course. They see the small revenue stream generated from these sales as supplementary. Libraries get the advantage of adding a great number of e-books to their collections at relatively low cost. When you are assessing the value of these collections, however, it may be more pertinent to look at the cost per use than the cost per title (Grigson 2009, 63). Generally, the included content is selected by the vendor or publisher, and libraries have no opportunity to shape the title lists. Sometimes content within these packages changes during the contract period, so libraries need to be aware of potential work involved in suppressing or adding MARC records to their systems. As with all subscription products, annual renewal costs can be problematic for libraries.

There are also subscription packages of newer content. The most widely adopted of these is probably O'Reilly's Safari product, which features computer guidebooks. In this model, new editions can replace old editions within the contract period and libraries have some control over title selection. The cost per title is significantly higher than that typically found in backlist subscription packages. Though annual renewal fees are still a burden, this is the type of content libraries weed and update frequently even in the print world.

From the vendor's point of view, subscriptions can be a challenge to sell because libraries frequently object to ongoing expenditures. If, however, the model is constructed so that the price per title is extremely low, it can make for an easy sale. To do this in a way that generates revenue is not easy. If the price per title hovers around $4 and the aggregator needs to cover sales and hosting costs, then the revenue to the publisher is necessarily less than 10 percent of its traditional expectation. Publishers would need to lease the title for at least ten years to see the same profit. For this reason, they are reluctant to include titles that still sell well in these packages.

Perpetual Ownership

Libraries can also choose to acquire e-books with the right to "perpetual access." This model is more aligned with traditional print collection practices in which libraries are building collections for future as well as current use. This model allows libraries to pay up front or over a couple of years for ongoing access to content. The price for this type of e-book purchase is typically higher than that for a print book. For single-title purchases, pricing can range from 20 to 100 percent higher than the cloth list price, depending on the vendor and type of access secured. Even single-user access almost always costs significantly more than the print list price. Preset e-book packages, frequently comprising all of a publisher's current content in a given subject area, can offer a savings over print. The cost can still be prohibitive, though, since libraries do not typically budget to purchase the complete frontlist of any academic publisher. On top of the e-book price, most aggregators charge libraries a platform maintenance fee, which is billed annually and is required for ongoing hosting of the e-books purchased.

Pay-per-View

Some aggregators and publishers also offer content on a pay-per-view or short-term rental basis. This can be a cost-effective way of providing access to e-book content. The library must be willing to accept ongoing fees, but it pays only for content being used. In 2007, short-term loan fees averaged between 10 and 15 percent of the total cost of the book. EBL, the predominant aggregator offering e-books through this model, gives libraries the option of automatically purchasing titles once they have been accessed a preset number of times (Chadwell 2009, 69).

In fiscal year 2007/8, the University of Texas at Austin devoted $300,000 to a pilot pay-per-view project with EBL. The library opted to pay for three views, with the fourth view triggering a purchase of the title.

Roughly two-thirds of the dollars allocated paid for views, and the remaining third went toward purchasing titles viewed four times. The library expended 95 percent of the dollars allocated (Macicak and Schell 2009). Interestingly, all of the titles selected for this study were from publishers whose output constituted less than 3 percent of the print approval plan and whose titles had below-average circulation rates in print. More about the University of Texas at Austin e-book program can be found in chapter 5.

LIBRARY ACQUISITION METHODS

Librarians can choose a variety of methods for acquiring e-books. Most e-book publishers, aggregators, and vendors offer methods that are familiar to selectors from their collection development work with print monographs: approval plans, firm orders, and standing orders. A few methods, however, are new to the electronic format: e-books acquired through subscription, through pay-per-view, and through patron-driven selection.

Approval Plan

Though aggregators and distributors have been notifying libraries of newly available e-books based on subject profiles for several years, true approval plan coverage of e-books, where books are "shipped" (activated) automatically and the library rejects unwanted titles, is now becoming available.

Libraries have the option to integrate their print and electronic monograph approval plans through their monograph aggregator or vendor. Libraries can choose to allow format duplication, effectively receiving both print and electronic versions of a given monograph (if both are available), or to set a preference for print or electronic format, based on factors such as subject, publication schedule, or type of e-book. For an e-book approval plan to be set fully in motion, new workflows need to be developed within the library to accommodate the approval and acquisition of e-book titles. Whereas print titles arriving on approval would normally be put onto viewing shelves and await a final decision by a selector librarian, thereafter moving through a physical receiving process—through cataloging, to preservation/physical processing for marking and stamping, and finally onto a library shelf for patron discovery—e-books "arriving" on approval need extra and special attention for final acquisition decisions and activation. In the e-book receiving process, there is no need for physical processing such as stamping and marking, so already the receiving process is streamlined. Once a selector has decided to add an e-book on approval to the library collection, the remaining receiving actions are centered around records work such as adding the MARC record to the library's catalog and ensuring that access is turned on for the library community at large. The latter activity involves adding the e-book URL to the catalog record as well as (if appropriate) activating the e-book on its platform in the library's link resolver (see below).

Traditional print vendors, however, see several challenges in adding e-book coverage to approval plans. As a rule, it is problematic to add any new data elements to approval systems. Doing so for elements such as binding type usually requires amending all existing plans, whether or not coverage for the new element is desired. In addition, effectively profiling an e-book requires descriptive parameters that do not exist in the print world. For instance, it is important to know if the e-book contains all of the content in the print book or, for example, if graphs and pictures have been left out. Ideally, approval plans also take into account digital rights management (DRM) parameters so that, for example, a profile might allow e-books only for titles that can be downloaded ten pages at a time or more and send slips for e-books with more restrictive printing options.

One of the primary differences between profiling an e-book and a print book is the lack of a physical item to hold and describe. Approval vendors have historically relied on the appearance of a physical book to trigger the profiling process. These books are ordered prepublication expressly for approval profiling. With e-books, vendors typically do not order new titles but rather accept metadata feeds from aggregators and publishers. As new titles come in from these feeds, e-books are profiled. Early profiling efforts have not consisted of book-in-hand description. Instead, e-books are linked with their print counterparts and assigned the same approval attributes automatically. To work accurately, vendors need access to full-text versions of the e-books they are describing, or else they must delay profiling the e-book until the print is available. As e-books are more frequently becoming available prior to their print counterparts, vendors have to find new ways to approach e-book profiling.

The biggest challenge in terms of managing workflow for the library is evaluating the e-book for selection. The arrival of an e-book on approval takes the form of the e-book being turned on or made accessible to the library for review. Whether this access is in the form of a full-book preview or by selected sections is up to the publisher. Librarians need to be able to evaluate the e-book in as complete a manner as possible and want to encourage publishers to provide complete access to the e-book content for selection purposes.

Delivering e-books on approval presents another new issue for print approval vendors, since there is not a physical item to send and fulfillment is largely out of their control. Vendors have had to develop back-end systems that notify e-book providers to turn on content for the appropriate library. Some vendors have built into this process a system that allows the library to review and reject content before invoicing.

Another complicating factor for vendors that provide approval services is that there are now multiple sources for the same content. Constructing systems that can automate selection while ordering e-books from multiple suppliers based on profiling tools is a challenge. Vendors face several difficult decisions. Should each aggregator's versions be profiled separately? Should vendors supply the first available edition on approval or incorporate wait times so a library can prefer one platform over another? How should vendors weigh price differences between platforms? The simple logic of most approval plan databases developed in the 1990s cannot easily be adjusted to accommodate such complex decision making.

One reason the development of e-book approval plans has been relatively slow is that historically there has been a significant delay between the availability of a print book and the availability of its e-book counterpart. This delay period is rapidly decreasing, but today only about 10 percent of print books handled on approval at Coutts Information Services have e-book alternates available at the time of profiling. However, libraries willing to wait ninety days from the date of print availability for an e-book may be able to get 30 percent of their approval content in e-format. Since publisher workflows for e-books are considerably different than their print workflows, it is unlikely the concurrency problem will be solved in the near term (Tian and Martin 2009, 74). Therefore, integrated print and e-book approval plans need to take into account a library's willingness to wait for an e-book when it is the preferred format. The best services will offer libraries the ability to vary wait times by publisher and subject area. They will also offer libraries a method for reviewing the titles on hold and forcing the available edition to ship.

Firm Order

Most full-service print vendors also offer libraries the ability to firm order e-books through their online ordering systems. Firm ordering of e-books can be on a single-title basis or can take the form of a selected package of titles. Since 2006, the appearance of e-books in online ordering databases has become commonplace, and the firm order process has become simple for libraries once they have completed license agreements with the e-book provider. For monograph vendors, the process of invoicing and supplying is completely different from that of print, since there is no physical item to ship and the process of turning titles on is handled by the e-book provider. The vendor must notify the e-book provider to turn on titles and invoice the library. Typically, the vendor also supplies a MARC record that includes the URL to the e-book.

For libraries, single-title e-book firm ordering is most efficiently accomplished through an e-book aggregator, though most publishers also offer the library the ability to direct order their e-books on a title-by-title basis. Most publishers also offer e-book packages, based on criteria such as subject or discipline, publication year, or others determined by the publisher or the library, which can be firm ordered direct with the publisher or through an e-book aggregator.

Patron-Driven Selection

Patron-driven (also known as patron-initiated) selection is an acquisition method that has been around since the early 2000s but is only now becoming a serious contender among the options available to libraries. Most e-book aggregators offer this acquisition model, and libraries are starting to see the value in it. The aggregator provides access to all e-book titles (or a selected group of titles, depending on how wide and deep the library intends its e-book collection to be); the library loads the associated MARC records into its catalog, thereby providing a discovery point; and the patron finds and accesses the e-book on the platform associated with the aggregator. After a predetermined number of visits, the library is billed for that title and from that point owns access to the title. The library works with the e-book aggregator to determine the limits for this program; limits can include the amount of money the library devotes to the program in a given amount of time, the most an e-book can cost to be included in the program, and the subjects or disciplines included in the program. For this acquisition method to be successful, the library should provide access not only from its own catalog but also from any other point of discovery advocated by the library—link resolvers, WorldCat, WorldCat Local, consortial catalogs, and the like. Some libraries find that the benefits of a patron-driven acquisition program—such as guaranteed use for every title purchased, automated acquisitions workflow, and instant access—outweigh the disadvantages, which are most often associated with the relatively smaller number of titles available for patron-driven acquisition, a resistance to change time-honored collection development practices, and a perceived loss of control over the title selection (and therefore spending practices) (Polanka 2009, 121).

Pay-per-View

Many e-book providers offer a pay-per-view option for acquisitions. This method is just how it sounds: the library pays on a view-by-view basis. E-book providers may charge a view in any one of several ways—by the chapter, by the book, or by the section. This can be a cost-effective method of providing access to e-book content. The library must be willing to accept ongoing fees, but it pays only for content being used. EBL is offering an acquisition method that combines the pay-per-view and patron-initiated models, in that the library pays a limited fee per patron use, and once the predetermined use threshold is reached the library pays the purchase price. Pay-per-view methods can also be a cost-effective way for libraries to fulfill interlibrary loan requests originating within their own institution, thereby eliminating the need to request a book from another library.

Standing Order

Print vendors have seen their standing order businesses erode since e-books have become the format of choice for many standing order titles. Libraries are generally pleased to have a vendor continue to manage the publisher relationship for them, but some publishers are reluctant to allow vendors this opportunity. When vendors are involved, they manage license negotiations, billing, tracking new editions, and problem solving if the library has difficulty accessing the content.

ACQUISITION ROUTES

Monograph vendors such as Coutts, YBP, Swets, Blackwell, and Baker and Taylor offer e-books for order and either provide access via their own vendor platform or are partnered with other e-book platform providers for access. A library places orders for e-books through a vendor system such as Swets's SwetsWise, YBP's GOBI, Blackwell's Online Bookshop, Baker and Taylor's Title Source 3, or Coutts's Oasis, just as it could with print. If using YBP or Blackwell, the library can choose among e-book provider platforms at the point of order; to date, YBP offers EBL, ebrary, and NetLibrary and Blackwell offers MyiLibrary, ebrary, and EBL. For Swets or Coutts, the e-book access platform is MyiLibrary. For the library to have access on a given platform, it may need to contact the platform provider and negotiate a license for access; this again depends on the provider and platform chosen by the library.

Libraries can also choose to purchase or subscribe to e-books directly through the publisher, where publishers are offering this option.

Publisher Direct

Some large publishers host their own electronic content and sell e-books directly to libraries. Frequently, publishers package e-books into collections and offer the packages at steeply discounted prices compared to print list prices. DRM on publisher sites can be more open than DRM on aggregator sites because the publishers are monitoring activity directly and can quickly pick up attempts at piracy. Publishers also feel more secure if a library has subscribed to a complete package of content. Some publishers, however, are unable or unwilling to sell individual titles to libraries (Worlock 2009). They do not offer the support of approval plans, and the quality of MARC records supplied varies greatly among publishers.

A Sampling of Vendors

Coutts www.couttsinfo.com

YBP www.ybp.com

Swets www.swets.com

Blackwell http://blackwellpublishing.com

Baker and Taylor www.btol.com

Vendor Online Ordering Systems

Coutts's Oasis http://couttsinfo.com/Services/oasis.htm

YBP's GOBI www.gobi3.com

Swets's SwetsWise www.swetswise.com

Blackwell's Online Bookshop http://bookshop.blackwell.co.uk

Baker and Taylor's Title Source 3 www.btol.com/ts3/

A Sampling of Publishers with E-book Platforms

Springer www.springer.com

Elsevier www.elsevier.com

Oxford University Press www.oup.com/online/

Royal Society of Chemistry www.rsc.org/publishing/ebooks/

Aggregator

Aggregators such as ebrary, EBL, NetLibrary, and Ingram Digital host and sell e-books from a wide range of publishers. They carry content available on publisher-direct sites as well as content from publishers that do not have their own hosting facilities. They may run promotions featuring reduced-price e-book packages consisting of content from one or from a variety of publishers. However, they are equipped to sell e-books title by title either directly or through a distributor such as a book vendor or subscription agent. Aggregators can help libraries simplify e-book acquisitions because they offer a single point of access through one license agreement. Similarly, aggregators offer the library the ability to purchase e-books from a wide variety of publishers in a one-stop shop. This can greatly reduce a library's workload searching for and selecting e-book content to acquire. However, some publishers hold back their most popular content from aggregators or disallow single-title sales of books in series. Other publishers bypass aggregators altogether, hoping to cut out the middleman.

Aggregators have to balance the needs of the libraries they sell to against the concerns of the publishers they represent. Aggregators would like to offer libraries the least restrictive access possible, but an open DRM policy may prevent a publisher from participating in an aggregator's program. Similarly, if the aggregator's business model does not offer a significant revenue stream for publishers, the aggregator will have difficulty attracting new publisher content.

Monograph Vendor

Most monograph vendors act merely as distributors for publishers and e-book aggregators. Still, they offer the advantage of ease of acquisition, since e-book ordering can occur alongside print ordering, and they can manage duplication between print and e-book editions. E-books can be purchased through their approval plans, and they have systems for notifying libraries of new e-books that meet their specifications. Monograph vendors also offer a single stream for invoicing and MARC records, which are usually of better quality than publisher MARC records.

ENSURING ACCESS

Simultaneous User Access Models

Early e-book products mimicked print workflows and structures, in part because convincing book publishers to make their content available any other way was inconceivable. As publishers have begun to see the financial advantages of moving libraries away from print and into e-books, they have become more willing to accommodate libraries' demands for simultaneous multiuser access. They do not, however, want to allow libraries to circumvent buying multiple copies of a title by opting for an e-book rather than print. Most publishers allow simultaneous use within the bounds of occasional use. Usage patterns that reflect use for a class demand higher access fees.

The most common options for the number of simultaneous users that can access an e-book at a time are single- and multiple-user access models.

In the single-user model, only one user can access an e-book at a time, and as the second and subsequent users attempt to access the e-book they are turned away. Multiple-user access models, by contrast, allow several or an unlimited number of users to access an e-book simultaneously. The multiple-user access model usually costs a bit more than the single-user model; for instance, ebrary typically charges 50 percent more for multiuser access. It is important for the library to consider the needs of its users when deciding between simultaneous user access models.

Some e-book providers handle access in a way that is more akin to print books, in that a user "checks out" a title for a given amount of time. This method is similar to the single-user access model, with the distinction that after the predetermined viewing period (akin to a circulation period for print books) has expired, the user no longer has access to the e-book. The providers who offer this method of access usually present the user with language that mimics print books—with links and tabs that are labeled "checkout" rather than "access." This access method is offered by OverDrive and NetLibrary and is based on a one book-one-reader framework, though some providers are starting to adopt the Amazon-style practice of allowing the user a preview of sections of the book (Bedord 2009, 16).

Devices and Readers

Vendors hosting e-books struggle with the wish to provide patrons all of the functionality the electronic format offers and the desire to avoid requiring users to download a reader to access the content. "Most campus libraries now host multiple e-book services for patrons, and each typically has its own e-reader application. These applications provide a range of functionality that can be applied to e-books, and new features, such as note sharing and rating, are being added all the time" (Nelson 2008, 50). However, given what is known about e-book usage, users get in and get out fairly quickly, and ease of access may trump features such as highlighting and note sharing. Since the library's electronic content is spread among many platforms, tools that facilitate research and study may be best hosted elsewhere.

Most users are familiar with proprietary e-book devices such as Kindle, nook, and Sony Reader. These are handheld devices through which a user can access an e-book store to purchase and download titles for reading directly on the device. Some libraries are experimenting with loaning e-book devices—preloaded with titles the library has purchased or to which it has subscribed—to their patrons as a form of e-book circulation. Princeton University launched its Kindle e-reader pilot program in Spring 2009, and on September 28 of that year students in three courses were given a new Kindle DX that contained their course readings for the semester.

The form of e-book access with which libraries are most familiar, however, is through a publisher or aggregator platform. Some examples include Coutts's MyiLibrary, NetLibrary, ebrary, and EBL. MyiLibrary and ebrary could be considered proprietary readers, in that they are platforms upon which e-books are hosted for viewing; it is not possible to view the e-books meant for these readers outside of the readers themselves. EBL and NetLibrary, acting as platforms or readers, on the one hand, also offer at least some of their titles as downloadable to an outside e-book reader device. A library that is building an e-book collection should consider the pros and cons of the various e-book devices and readers available, which method of access would most benefit its users, and whether the library is interested in or able to lend e-book devices to its users.

Perpetual Access

Archiving is currently a significant issue for libraries and vendors involved in supplying perpetual access to e-books. Creating a viable infrastructure for securing ongoing access in the face of a corporate failure is considered a top priority by libraries, publishers, and vendors alike. Many research libraries are reluctant to move into collecting e-books until a solution has been reached.

WORKFLOW AND PROCESS

As new formats emerge, libraries must be able to adjust their workflows, policies, and procedures to reflect the change. E-book workflows can be built on print book models to a point, but libraries must recognize that the difference in format requires a new stream for processing, and this requires the library to create new procedures for handling e-books, from evaluation to activation and most stops in between.

Evaluation

Most vendors and publishers provide libraries some opportunity to view at least portions of their content before committing to a purchase. One of the benefits of acquiring digital resources is the library's ability to have temporary access—a trial—with which to determine whether the resource should be added to the collection. Most vendors are willing to give libraries limited time trials of their products. Trials may be password based or via IP authentication.

Previewing e-book content can take the form of a "see inside the book" feature (most people are familiar with this from ordering print books online) or access to portions of or the full text of the e-book for a limited amount of time. This is especially important if libraries are buying e-books on a nonreturnable basis.

Licensing

Licenses are a major concern for libraries for all electronic resource acquisitions. The library is responsible for initiating a license negotiation, and the burden falls on the library to negotiate a license that meets its requirements (Algenio and Thompson-Young 2005, 119). Many libraries are still working to finalize a workflow for managing the licensing process, whether for e-books, e-serials, or databases. Libraries have come to expect that when they are subscribing to journals—title by title or in packages—or databases, they must negotiate and execute a license agreement with each publisher before access is granted. Serials vendors are not in the habit of handling licensing agreements on behalf of libraries; as a matter of fact, most serials vendors do not require the library to report on the license status to place an order. The library is responsible for contacting the publisher and starting the license negotiation. Most libraries would probably agree that it is better to conduct the negotiation and execute the license before placing a final order for a product. After all, if a library and a publisher were not able to reach an agreement, it would be fruitless to order and pay for the resource. All the same is true for e-book acquisitions.

If a library is dealing with the publisher directly, whether to acquire a single e-book title or an e-book package, the license process must be incorporated into the acquisitions workflow. Many publishers allow one license agreement to be executed with a library—for the first title or package acquisition—and thereafter implement addendums or amendments for each subsequent acquisition. Do not be surprised, however, if some publishers require separately executed license agreements for each acquisition. Libraries should complete the license negotiation with a publisher before issuing a purchase order or finalizing the order, in keeping with the library's internal acquisitions policy.

Libraries that build their e-book collections by using an e-book aggregator see a somewhat streamlined license process. Many e-book aggregators require the library to sign a license agreement with them, and they in turn handle the license agreements with their publishers, thereby eliminating the need for the library to negotiate and execute a license with each separate publisher. The e-book aggregators who offer this method of license management are certainly more attractive to libraries as partners in building an e-book collection. Libraries need to be aware, though, that this is a third-party method of licensing and that the aggregator needs to fulfill its obligation to have all agreements in place with the publishers to ensure protection for the library against third-party claims of copyright or other usage rights infringement. When negotiating an agreement with an e-book aggregator, the library should ensure that a clause exists in the license that guarantees that the licensor (the e-book aggregator) has agreements in place with each publisher with which it deals.

Title Selection

As primitive as it sounds, bibliographers still commonly use Excel spreadsheets to review e-books for selection, since few have truly incorporated e-books into their regular workflows. Bibliographers request title lists from their e-book vendors, delete unwanted titles, and return the edited list to initiate an order. As more e-book aggregators integrate their e-book offerings into their print book online ordering systems, however, libraries will be able to redesign their e-book workflow to make the process more automated and less labor intensive.

Approval plans. Approval plans that integrate e-book and print book coverage are just now hitting the market. To be of much use, they must take into account that print books and e-books rarely become available concurrently. Libraries that prefer to work with an e-book provider that is not distributed by their primary print vendor may separate out the subjects for which they prefer e-book coverage and use another vendor for e-book approvals. Many libraries use their approval plans to generate notification slips for newly available e-books. Vendors are seeing an increased demand for plans that help them manage this growing stream of content. Libraries are experimenting with managing e-book approval plans alongside their print approval plans. Of concern for libraries is the publication delay; libraries are asking e-book approval plan providers to build a system whereby it is possible to indicate that the library prefers one format over another given a specific publication schedule parameter. For instance, the library might prefer the e-book format if the e-book is released within sixty days of print, but if the e-book is not released within sixty days then it would prefer print to be shipped instead.

Patron selection. Patron-driven collection development is becoming increasingly popular in U.S. libraries, and e-books make this type of collecting feasible. Several e-book aggregators offer this type of service. Typically, libraries fill out a simple profile identifying their collecting interests. The vendor supplies MARC records for titles that meet the library's criteria and makes the e-books accessible to the library. The library loads the records into its catalog but pays only for titles that get used. Sometimes the library pays for a short-term loan prior to triggering a purchase (see the discussion of pay-per-view under "Library Acquisition Methods"). In other models, purchase is triggered by a set number of uses. This can simplify selecting and acquiring e-books for the library, especially if it is able to work with a one-line invoice for content. Libraries that are heavily dependent on fund codes to manage their budgets may find this type of collecting problematic unless they restrict the program to one subject area. Future iterations of this model may better facilitate fund accounting.

The main objection to this method of e-book acquisition is cost. Some early adopters of this type of program found it extremely popular with their patrons, and they quickly exhausted their funds for e-books. Costs can be managed by limiting the number and types of titles available through a patron-selection program (Chadwell 2009, 72). Libraries can set an upper limit on the cost of any book as a parameter in their patron-driven selection plan, thereby decreasing the chances that largely expensive titles deplete the available funds and ensuring that the library gets the most e-book for every dollar spent.

Ordering

Libraries can firm order e-books using the same processes they use to acquire print books. As more vendors and aggregators incorporate their e-books into online ordering systems, libraries can create workflows that resemble their print firm order workflows, but adjusted to account for the activation process rather than the receiving process. Working within the vendor's or aggregator's online ordering system, libraries identify titles and either order directly through the online system or download MARC records and create purchase orders within their ILS. These databases offer much richer information than can be offered in an Excel spreadsheet, and frequently they provide access to the e-book text for bibliographer review. They also offer the opportunity to view the library's history with other editions of the title easily.

Receipt: Activating Access

Though the ordering process for e-books may tend to mirror that already established for print book ordering, at the point of receipt the formats' workflows diverge completely. The library relies heavily on vendor or publisher notification that a title has been activated on the e-book platform. If the vendor or publisher is unable or unwilling to provide access notification, the library must proactively check for access on a routine basis, which can disrupt the workflow. The library also relies on the publisher or vendor to provide an appropriate URL for accessing the title. At the point that access has been activated on the platform, the library can in turn provide access within its systems—in its OPAC, through its link resolver, on subject guides. Depending on local practices, after activation the e-book record can then be fully cataloged.

Perpetual Access

Ensuring access to resources to which the library has devoted valuable funds is a fundamental concern. In the print world, this involves physically preserving the material for future use. In the digital world, the act of preservation is quite a bit more complicated. The infrastructure in place for ensuring access to electronic serials—through Portico and LOCKSS, for example—is being adapted to accommodate e-book content for preservation. Libraries and e-book providers and publishers will need to work together to develop methods by which libraries can preserve the e-book content for which they have purchased perpetual access rights. Portico and LOCKSS are discussed further in chapter 7. As digital preservation systems are developed for e-books, libraries will need to create workflows around the processes involved in contributing content for perpetual access.

E-BOOK LICENSING

Libraries have become well versed in the digital age at negotiating licenses for most electronic resource acquisitions. E-book licensing presents similar issues to that encountered when licensing other electronic content, such as e-journals and databases. The information contained within this section is meant to help libraries understand some of the bigger issues they are likely to encounter when negotiating licensing with e-book providers and in no way should be construed to be legal advice. If in doubt about local policy and practice, consult the legal counsel for your institution.

Indemnification

Whether you are licensing e-books from a publisher or an aggregator, it is important for the licensor to indemnify the library against third-party claims of infringement of copyright or any other rights arising out of the library's use of the e-book. This ensures that, if a publisher or other copyright holder claims that the library should not actually have rights to use the content provided by the licensor, the library cannot be accused of copyright infringement (as long as the use abides by the terms of the license, and the terms of the license are in keeping with copyright laws).

A licensor may ask a library to agree to indemnify the licensor against misuse (or abuse) by the library's authorized users. A library needs to be careful not to accept an indemnification clause that requires the library to indemnify the licensor against use by their patrons. A library can agree elsewhere in the license to take all reasonable measures to protect the licensed materials from misuse and to inform its users about the rights and restrictions they have in using the licensed materials. A library will, however, find it difficult to offer any kind of guarantee that its users will not abuse their rights and should not accept responsibility beyond due diligence.

Interlibrary Loan

E-book ILL remains an unresolved issue. Publishers and aggregators generally agree with libraries that sharing monographs is covered under "fair-use" protections, but without the inherent limits of a physical item to prevent extreme sharing, publishers fear ILL of e-books will ruin them financially. Publishers and aggregators recognize the value of ILL and are working with libraries to create a system that allows e-books to be shared between institutions.

Libraries struggle not only with fulfilling ILL requests for users from other libraries (which is part of the goodwill libraries foster in their communities) but also with retrieving material through ILL requests on behalf of their own patrons. Some publishers think that once a library has purchased an e-book it cannot restrict ILL per se, though these publishers are not the norm. Those publishers who can agree to permit ILL often greatly restrict the portion of the licensed material that can be used to fulfill ILL requests as well as the form of delivery. For instance, ebrary (as an aggregator) has negotiated contracts with some publishers who agree that a library should be able to engage in ILL with its e-book content, but the license between ebrary and the library states that ILL can be fulfilled only by printing content from the e-book to be sent by any means—fax, post, even e-mail (if the library wants to take the time to scan in the content that was printed from a digital file). The ebrary platform has a printing limit, so logically the library can only print pages up to the limit in any session, making it difficult to fulfill ILL for an entire book. Those library users who need access to an entire e-book through ILL will be disappointed to find that their library can acquire only sections of the book at a time.

At least one e-book provider—EBL—offers libraries a pay-per-view model for using e-books (see "Library Acquisition Methods"). This method could be used to fulfill ILL requests made by the library's own users. Instead of searching for another library that owns the title and requesting it via ILL from that library, the home library could purchase

Licensee

The person or entity that receives permission under a License to access or use digital information. The Licensee, often a library, educational, or research organization, generally pays the Licensor a fee for permission to use digital information.

Licensor

The person or entity that gives or grants a License. The Licensor owns or has permission to distribute digital materials to a Licensee. If it is representing the interests of copyright owners in a License Agreement, the Licensor must have the financial means and legal authority to provide the services to which the parties agreed under the License Agreement.

Indemnity

One party's obligation to insure, shield, or otherwise defend another party against a third-party's claims that result from performance under, or breach of, the agreement.

SOURCE: YALE UNIVERSITY LIBRARY, LIBLICENSE

limited-time access to the title and allow the user access for the designated time. The advantages could include some cost savings in terms of ILL processing; the price per view of a title accessed on pay-per-view is typically a fraction of the publisher list price, and the workload on the library would be less than with traditional ILL request and fulfillment. Compare that to the typical staff costs and fees associated with ILL request and fulfillment, and the library could see some reduction in expenditure for ILL processing.

Another possible solution is to allow libraries to fulfill ILL requests at the article or chapter level, if such are assigned digital object identifiers, either with a limited-time access model as mentioned or via an electronic document delivery system. This method would bypass printing limits, serve to ease the concern of publishers about widespread distribution of content, and allow libraries to continue providing a vital service to their patrons as well as patrons of other libraries.

Whatever the policy of the e-book publisher or aggregator, the license agreement should reflect the level of ILL permission under which the library can expect to operate. Because this is such a sensitive issue on both sides, it might be best to have clear language describing the methods that are permitted as well as those that are restricted rather than rely on vague language that leaves much to interpretation.

Usage Rights and Restrictions

Usage rights and restrictions for a single title may differ greatly depending upon where it is hosted. Publisher sites tend to be the most open, for they trust themselves to catch acts of piracy, and maintaining open DRM allows them to differentiate themselves in the marketplace from other publishers and e-book aggregators.

Restrictions on aggregator sites are being lifted as the relationships between publishers and distributors are maturing. However, "the realm of fair use is, perhaps, the most polarizing force between libraries and publishers. Academic libraries, by virtue of their location, are both the beneficiaries and conduits of this privilege. As information providers, libraries' missions are about unfettered access for educational advancement. Publishers, in the other corner of the boxing ring, are determined to control and protect their intellectual property" (Algenio and Thompson-Young 2005, 120). Still, the more restrictive the access, the easier it is for a distributor to attract publisher content. Publishers are more likely to agree to offer their content to customers through an aggregator if the aggregator can offer a degree of protection in the form of a DRM system. However, even publishers that do not have their own sites are beginning to understand that if DRM restrictions render a book virtually unusable, there will be little revenue generated from e-book sales (Worlock 2009). A delicate balance therefore must be struck between usability and protection.

Libraries, of course, want the broadest usage rights possible. They want their patrons to be able to download sections for personal use; to print multiple pages of the e-book; and to be able to use the e-book content for academic, research, and scholarly pursuits, which may include digitally collating the content for use in course packs and course reserves and sharing minimal, insubstantial portions of content with research partners outside of their home institution. Libraries also want permission to create backup copies of content, consistent with their preservation mission. Depending upon the library's legal point of view, it may sometimes be more advantageous to have these rights spelled out in the license, at other times preferable to simply have a fair-use statement in the license—broad and open to interpretation.

E-BOOK CATALOGING

It has become the industry standard for e-book suppliers to provide free MARC records with each purchase. In part this practice grew out of the need to provide the library with a URL pointing to the purchased title. Free MARC records sometimes consist of only basic bibliographic information such as ISBN and title along with the URL. Others may conform to the PCC Guide for Aggregator Vendors (Culbertson et al. 2009).

Vendors struggle to balance the desire to provide a high-quality product that reflects well on the organization and the need to provide e-book records cost effectively. Creating good MARC records for large publisher packages is a complex exercise. Frequently, publisher-supplied records are of little use, and vendors mine print records to populate e-book records. Issues arise when publishers reuse ISBNs, provide URLs that point to the wrong content, or are not clear about which titles are included in a given package sale.

In August 2009, the Program for Cooperative Cataloging provider-neutral practice for cataloging electronic monographs went into effect. With this practice in place, there is no longer a need for separate OCLC records for each e-book provider; rather, OCLC e-book records are provider neutral, which means that no provider information need appear anywhere in the OCLC record (e.g., in the 5xx notes fields, the 7xx added-entry fields, or the 856 electronic access fields). The provider-neutral e-book record can be downloaded into the library's catalog for use with any entity providing access to that e-book; in other words, the library can customize it as necessary after it is downloaded to the local system. The practice thereby eases the library's burden of finding an appropriate OCLC catalog record for each e-book provider through which it might have access to a particular e-book title. On a local level (and if appropriate within local policies), libraries are able to include all e-book access points on a single record rather than have multiple records in their system for the same title, each with different access points. In terms of ordering and receiving, this practice reduces time spent trying to find an appropriate OCLC record for a particular provider. In terms of cataloging, the practice reduces the time spent repeatedly cataloging a title that might have multiple access points. Finally, in terms of discoverability, the practice means that, when a user finds the e-book title in the library's OPAC or through the link resolver, all access points display within the same item, thereby conveying to the user in a cleaner manner that a particular title might be available through a variety of access points.

E-BOOKS AND ERMS

An electronic resources management system (ERMS) is software that helps a library manage the details related to its subscriptions to electronic content. Since the management of electronic resources differs from the management of print resources in almost every way, new systems have been developed to facilitate the workflow and ease the burden of managing licenses, holdings, renewals, and usage statistics. Though originally designed to deal with article content delivered in e-journals and databases that aggregate collections of e-journals, the library can customize its ERMS to accommodate its e-book collection as well (see Breeding 2008).

Managing Packages versus Single Titles

By the very nature of package pricing, libraries tend to dedicate larger amounts of their materials budget to e-book packages and relatively less on single-title e-book orders. Whether purchased or subscribed, e-book packages can be handled in an ERMS much the same as e-journal packages—that is, the source of the order (the resource), the license details, and renewal information can all refer to the package while the individual titles contained within the package constitute the holdings and are that upon which the usage statistics are gathered and stored.

With the growing use of approval plans and patron-driven acquisition methods, however, libraries are beginning to shift their funding focus to acquiring e-books that are not part of a package. An important decision in the ERMS implementation process is how to handle these individual titles. If the library is acquiring e-books direct from a publisher, one option is to treat the publisher as the resource and source of the license and to include every title obtained from that publisher as a holding. Usage statistics—whether gathered from the publisher or the platform provider—can then be stored in the ERMS and used to calculate cost per use for the titles from that publisher. If a library is acquiring e-books from an aggregator, another option is to treat the aggregator as the resource and source of the license (if such is the case) and to include every title obtained from that aggregator as a holding. Usage statistics—whether gathered from the aggregator, the platform provider, or the publisher—can then be stored in the ERMS and used to calculate cost per use for the titles acquired through that aggregator.

Cost-per-Use Statistical Analysis

A key function of an ERMS is the automation of gathering and storing usage statistics and calculating cost per use. As long as the e-book provider is able to supply usage statistics for the library, this functionality can be applied to e-books as well.

License Management

E-book licenses need to be managed just as e-journal or database licenses do, and the ERMS is designed to provide a system for managing the life cycle of license agreements. In determining whether to set up the ERMS for the e-book acquisition at the package, publisher, or aggregator level, a library might consider the licensor as the determining factor. For instance, if the library is acquiring e-books through an approval plan with an aggregator, and the aggregator is the licensor, then the ERMS records should probably be set up with the aggregator as the resource. Thereafter, any e-book orders through that aggregator can be linked to the aggregator resource record, and the license agreement can be coded and entered into the ERMS as a license record linked to that resource. Similarly, if the library is acquiring e-books (as a package or title by title) direct from the publisher (who in this case would be the licensor), the ERMS records could reflect the publisher as the resource, and the license agreement and the e-book package order would be linked to the publisher resource record.

> Monitoring the adoption of e-books and the nature of e-book use by users/readers/consumers is crucial, since this will have consequences for, among other things, the role of libraries as intermediaries, pricing strategies and the viability of e-book publishers and distributors, e-book distribution channels, and copyright and licensing regulation.
>
> (VASILEIOU ET AL. 2009, 190)

The ERMS is designed to manage the life cycle of the e-book license. This includes documenting the effective date of the license, which is useful in tracking the negotiation process; documenting the expiration date, which is useful in managing renewals if the product is subscription based; and documenting the terms of use rights and restrictions included in the license. Most ERMSs provide a public display option, allowing the library to convey to the end user the rights and restrictions for using the electronic product. Some libraries also use the ERMS to provide a hyperlink to the actual license agreement—usually redacted to remove sensitive or confidential information—stored on the library's server. In terms of due diligence, both of these functions serve to fulfill the library's obligation to convey to its users the terms and conditions by which their use of the electronic product is governed.

CONCLUSION

As libraries move forward and begin to build their e-book collections in earnest, the processes by which those e-books make it from the publisher to the end user will become the mainstream, and the processes that governed print book acquisitions will no longer be the norm or even the foundation upon which e-book procedures are built. Whatever the outcome of the ongoing discussions about workflow, acquisition procedures, and licensing, e-books are here to stay. Standards for e-book format and metadata will continue to evolve, and staff will need to be retrained to adapt not only to conversion but to creation of e-book metadata. As more publishers offer their content as e-books, libraries will need to forge new partnerships and license agreements, and the day-to-day management of the life cycle of an e-book will fall to a wider set of staff than currently devoted to electronic resource management. This could mean cross-training or retraining existing staff and expanding or merging organizational units. Whatever the future holds for e-book acquisitions, the library will be at the center, ready and willing to adapt to the challenges.

In the meantime, it would be a mistake for libraries to allow current print workflows to drive e-book acquisition strategies. Purchasing e-books is a complex endeavor, and unlike print books the product varies depending on the source. Many people within the library community have a stake in the process, and choices made may have a profound impact on the success of the library.

REFERENCES

Algenio, Emilie, and Alexia Thompson-Young. 2005. "Licensing E-books: The Good, the Bad, and the Ugly." *Journal of Library Administration* 42 (3): 113–128.

Bedord, J. 2009. "Ebooks Hit Critical Mass: Where Do Libraries Fit with Oprah?" *Online* 33 (3): 14.

Breeding, Marshall. 2008. "Helping You Buy Electronic Resource Management Systems." *Computers in Libraries* 28 (7): 6–96.

Chadwell, Faye A. 2009. "What's Next for Collection Management and Managers? User-Centered Collection Management." *Collection Management* 34 (2): 69.

Culbertson, Becky, Yael Mandelstam, and George Prager. 2009. *Provider-Neutral E-monograph MARC Record Guide.* Washington, D.C.: Program for Cooperative Cataloging, www.loc.gov/catdir/pcc/bibco/PN-Guide.pdf.

Grigson, Anna. 2009. "Evaluating Business Models for E-books through Usage Data Analysis: A Case Study from the University of Westminster." *Journal of Electronic Resources Librarianship* 21 (1): 62.

Macicak, Susan, and Lindsey Schell. 2009. "Case Study: Patron Driven Purchasing at UTA. *Ebook Library Blog,* August 19, http://blog.eblib .com/?s=macicak.

Nelson, Mark R. 2008. "E-books in Higher Education: Nearing the End of the Era of Hype?" *EDUCAUSE Review* 43 (2).

Polanka, Sue. 2009. "Off the Shelf: Patron-Driven Acquisition." *Booklist* 105 (1): 121.

Tian, Xuemei, and Bill Martin. 2009. "Business Models in Digital Book Publishing: Some Insights from Australia." *Publishing Research Quarterly* 25 (2): 73–78.

Vasileiou, Magdalini, Richard Hartley, and Jennifer Rowley. 2009. "An Overview of the E-book Marketplace." *Online Information Review* 33 (1): 173–192.

Worlock, Kate. 2009. "E-books Market Size, Share and Forecast Report." *In Outsell Market Intelligence Service: Market Size, Share and Forecast Report,* vol. 3. Burlingame, Calif.: Outsell.

7

The Use and Preservation of E-books

ALICE CROSETTO

When e-books began to gain prominence in the 1990s, some librarians remained firmly entrenched in the print world; others hastened into the digital world, never looking back and hoping that any perceived negative baggage associated with print would not pertain to the e-book. However, after twenty years, librarians are discovering that the challenges once thought to be associated exclusively with the print monograph are, in fact, applicable to the e-book: availability of funds and escalating costs, equitable distribution of titles among subject areas, use statistics, and preservation. Though budgeting funds and addressing curricular and patron needs remain high priorities, e-book use appears to have captivated the interest of librarians, as evidenced in the literature. Patron use continues to be one of the most concrete factors that prove the value of library resources. The collection of e-book use data and their subsequent analysis are important for librarians worldwide. If a greater percentage of acquisitions funds are shifting to the e-book format, then librarians need to be able to prove that this investment is worthwhile. Libraries facing monetary issues are forced to consider and implement serious reductions in staff, open hours, and resources. As library support and services, especially resources, become more virtual, funds still need to be allocated to purchase and maintain the virtual environment. Librarians in all types of libraries need to justify the expense of e-books. Producing use data for both e-books and print is of paramount importance in this climate.

Preservation of and perpetual access to e-books are interconnected issues of great importance to librarians. They already face difficult questions about superseded e-books, such as the fate of last year's directory or the final location of an authoritative encyclopedia's first edition when the second edition arrives. Currently, librarians have no guidelines or standards to consult about what file format will be supported in the future for both storage and access. Moreover, as companies consolidate, what becomes of the content and interfaces librarians and end users rely upon? Guaranteeing that safeguards are in place to access and preserve electronic content is paramount, particularly in the academic library setting, where e-books may need to be kept accessible indefinitely. As the e-book format continues to rise in importance in all libraries, librarians and other interested parties need to address the preservation of e-books just as they have with print.

E-BOOK DELIVERY METHODS AND USE REPORTS

Understanding what constitutes the relevant use of the data remains challenging. Since e-book delivery varies, via either an e-book reader or the Web, e-book data vary. For the e-book reader, does a use mean a checkout of the piece of equipment, or does each accessed file on the device constitute a use? One reader may have numerous e-book files, so is the circulation use one or is it five (representing the number of e-books on the reader)? As for the e-book delivered via the Web, which is more common at the academic level, several use variables are possible such as clicking on the file, downloading the file, searching the file, or time spent viewing the file.

E-book delivery via the Web remains the primary model studied in the literature, possibly because this method offers more challenges than its handheld alternate. As more patrons become comfortable with and accustomed to accessing resources on the Internet, the increase in this form of delivery will force librarians to address analyzing use statistics. Typically, a library's ILS is able to generate use statistics. This use data parallel their print counterpart. More accurate and detailed reporting of e-book use is generated by the vendor that supplied the e-book, which most librarians prefer, but this presents difficulties in that each vendor generates unique use reports; even a basic data point such as use is subject to each vendor's interpretation. Given these issues, the establishment of a standardization body was inevitable.

Standardization of E-book Use Statistics

As more librarians realized that consistency in e-book use statistics was a priority and vendors responded to their customers' needs, several initiatives were set in place. Project COUNTER (Counting Online Use of Networked Electronic Resources), launched in March 2002, is an international initiative serving librarians, publishers, and intermediaries. This collaboration sets the standards that facilitate the recording and reporting of online use statistics in a consistent, credible, and compatible way. This not-for-profit organization, based in the United Kingdom, has sponsored numerous research projects that will shed light on use-related research and services. Complete reports on these projects are accessible on COUNTER's website (www.projectcounter.org). COUNTER's future objectives as listed on its homepage may reap even more rewards, such as improving the reliability of the core COUNTER data, increasing the number of COUNTER-compliant vendors, and working with other industry organizations to provide practical value data (based on COUNTER codes) to librarians and vendors.

COUNTER's early success was built on the earlier work of the International Coalition of Library Consortia (ICOLC). Established in 1997 as an informal, self-organizing group of 150 library consortia worldwide, ICOLC primarily serves its members by facilitating discussion of issues of common interest. By the late 1990s, ICOLC guidelines for statistical measures were compiled, providing vendors with a practical framework in which to deliver use statistics to consortium administrators who needed this information (Cox 2007). ICOLC identified key elements of use reports such as numbers of sessions, searches, menu selections, full-content units accessed, and turnaways. Some publishers became ICOLC compliant, but the fact that ICOLC guidelines were not mandatory allowed personal interpretation by individual vendors. Nevertheless, COUNTER has taken the lead in providing reliable, standardized, electronic statistics.

A second initiative is the Standardized Use Statistics Harvesting Initiative (SUSHI, www.niso.org/workrooms/sushi) protocol, which consolidates vendor use data (Cox 2007). SUSHI is in fact an initiative of the National Information Standards Organization (NISO), which was founded in 1939 and continues to identify, develop, maintain, and publish technical standards for both traditional and new technologies. According to its online documentation, SUSHI protocol defines an automated request and response model for the harvesting of electronic resource use data utilizing a web services framework. It is intended to replace the time-consuming user-mediated collection of use data reports.

Available Data

The benefits of COUNTER are many, but for most collection development librarians the two most important benefits are the standardization of use data from vendors and data reports. Easy-to-read and easy-to-understand reports help the librarian with collection questions. COUNTER provides the following data:

- number of successful requests by month and title
- number of successful section requests by month and title
- number of turnaways by month and title
- number of turnaways by month and service
- number of searches and sessions by month and title
- total number of searches and sessions by month and service

As with the use data for print titles supplied by the ILS, COUNTER reports provide the collection development librarian with the necessary information for making decisions, such as whether purchased items are being used, what areas need additional titles, and which titles are not being used. Beyond these basic data points, current database technology can generate data from electronic resources previously unavailable from print resources; for example, unique data available from COUNTER include tracking which sections have been accessed. For an e-book, this means which chapters have been viewed, and for the e-reference work which specific entries have been viewed. Knowing what topics are being viewed in reference works can point the collection development librarian in the direction of needed resources. Additional information that can be easily gleaned from this data is which vendor is providing the most-used titles. If collection development librarians want this comparable information from the print resources, they must continually generate ILS lists and export the data into spreadsheets. When funds are tight, the librarian who has cost-per-use data at hand can easily justify maintaining and expanding these electronic resources and the vendors who provide the titles most used by patrons, and can thus plan purchasing accordingly.

As NISO and COUNTER further their collaborative efforts in the delivery of standardized use statistics to librarians and vendors, recent years have seen the need to identify even more quantitative e-book use data. One such endeavor is under way in the United Kingdom by the Joint Information Systems Committee, better known as JISC. The JISC National E-books Observatory Project was set up to perform what its name suggests: to observe the impact and behaviors of those using e-books and to find innovative methods to encourage e-book production. Just as in the United States, JISC knew that since the demand for providing textbooks in the electronic format was growing, all interested individuals wanted the facts, namely, what the impact would be on print sales and how much should be charged for providing e-textbooks.

One additional use element now available from electronic resources is deep-log analysis (DLA). Grigson (2009) has identified the need for DLA, which produces a better understanding of e-book use based on a more detailed set of quantitative data. DLA produces raw data detailing how users navigate through e-books. Pairing this data with user characteristics as well as institutional profiles and patterns produces an accurate accounting of e-book use. Results from JISC's groundbreaking 2007/8 DLA study will undoubtedly be used to set the standards for future study. Once this study is fully analyzed and its findings understood, librarians will have a better understanding of how users use e-books. Both Cox's (2007) detailed account of DLA in his discussion of CIBER and the JISC National E-books Observatory Project website (www.jiscebooksproject.org) provide additional current information, well worth reading.

Understanding the Data

The standardization of e-book use statistics in recent years illustrates the power of librarians and their ability to be the driving factors in obtaining what is needed in order to be responsive to their patrons and responsible for their resources. Once librarians have the use statistics for e-books, the next step traditionally involves analyzing the data.

Early and recent studies reveal what and how e-books are being used, often in comparison to print resources. Christianson and Aucoin (2005) discovered in their subject analysis that certain LC classification ranges showed definite preference in format. For example, items in the LC classification range B for Philosophy were clearly used predominantly in print, whereas the LC classification range Z (Bibliography. Library Science. Information Resources [General]) items showed more use in the e-book format. Recently, Slater (2009) finds similar results: print appears to be the preferred format for humanities subject areas, and the e-book format is preferred for the sciences.

Regardless of the numerous stellar studies, how e-books are used and to what extent patrons are reading and understanding the content remain as puzzling as how to extract this same information regarding patrons reading the print book. A patron checks out a print book, but is there a guarantee that she read the entire book? Did she just flip through a couple of pages, glancing at a few images or text sections before returning the item? Most librarians would be content that the library resource is in the hands of a patron, because this represents a successful decision in acquisitions. Should this attitude be transferred to e-book use? As long as the e-book is accessed, does this not also represent a successful decision? Currently, with dwindling funds for all library resources, used or circulated items validate collection development decisions. However, possibly because of the relative newness of e-books, or the increasing ability to identify and analyze electronic data, librarians have spent a considerable amount of research regarding the patron use of the e-book.

Littman and Connaway (2004) found that patrons use e-books differently than print books; for example, e-books were used for quick reference and print books were used for intensive reading. The more recent study of Noorhidawati and Gibb (2008) presents one of the most thorough analyses of student perception and reaction to the e-book. The three primary purposes identified for using e-books are listed in order of popularity, number one being the most popular: (1) finding relevant content, which involves searching e-book content for relatively moderate relevant sections of information; (2) fact finding, which involves using the e-book to find a specific piece of information; and (3) extended reading, which involves reading larger sections such as chapters as well as the e-book in its entirety. Noorhidawati and Gibb's research is compelling and should encourage others to replicate this study at their own libraries as a means to justify current e-book collections and future purchases.

Several studies reveal the e-book features that make this format more attractive to a user, including 24/7 accessibility, multiple-user ability (provided this platform is available and purchased), capability to print selections, ability to search within the document, and availability of out-of-print titles. At the same time, the e-book format is not without concerns for the reader. Several recent studies address the patron's attitude toward using e-books, especially Gregory (2008) and Noorhidawati and Gibb (2008). The latter reported that 94 percent of respondents preferred to use a printed book for extended reading and that many respondents indicated that reading on-screen for extended periods was uncomfortable. The former provides a more balanced interpretation of the attitudes found among the undergraduates at the author's institute. Gregory utilized first-hand observations and interactions of the librarians as well as a survey for her study. She noted a reluctance to use e-books found in the catalog and negative comments that culminated with a patron proclaiming to the librarian, "But I want a real book." Gregory also found that 66 percent of students surveyed preferred to use a physical book. It will be interesting to see if her findings are substantiated in further research regarding students' attitudes of print and electronic resources.

PRESERVATION

E-books cannot be lost on the way to school, torn by the dog, or accidentally dropped in a tubful of water by a mischievous younger sibling. All the same, e-books, whether those with little to no use or those with outdated content, cannot occupy valuable server space ad perpetuum. Damaged print resources are traditionally withdrawn, and low-use items are often retired to remote storage facilities, if available. In some situations, patrons can visit the off-site facility and have access to the resources, or they can request that items be returned to the home library for checkout. This is not, however, the case with electronic resources. How can individual libraries preserve their digital collections? Will electronic content always be accessible? Considering the time, expense, and necessary technological support, most libraries have to look outside their own walls to address the needs for the preservation of electronic resources.

Librarians employ Plato's often-quoted text, "Necessity is the mother of invention," and do what they naturally do best—build networking structures and entities. Preserving electronic resources has been addressed for some time. LOCKSS (Lots of Copies Keep Stuff Safe, www.clockss.org), established in the early 2000s and based at Stanford University Libraries, is an open-source software program that provides librarians with an easy and inexpensive means of preserving local copies of authorized content. Another initiative established about the same time for the preservation of scholarly literature is Portico (www.portico.org), the electronic-archiving initiative created by JSTOR. Responding to the needs of libraries and publishers and knowing that the complexity of preserving core electronic scholarly literature required optimal collaboration, the Portico project staff designed the technology necessary to accomplish its archival services. As of summer 2009, almost five hundred libraries and over six thousand e-book titles are associated with Portico.

Librarians and publishers have taken electronic preservation one step further—the creation of a geographically distributed dark archive for the preservation of academic publications. CLOCKSS (Controlled LOCKSS) has been established to ensure that the digital collections of today are available for future generations. In a dark archive, access to the resources is either extremely limited or totally restricted, which guarantees that the resources are safe. Beginning in October 2008, CLOCKSS has been building itself into the premier archive for web-based scholarly resources on a global level. The involvement of individuals who are making electronic preservation a priority, namely, librarians and publishers, should guarantee its success. As the primary governing agents, librarians and publishers are in the best positions to set policies, standards, and practices as well as to maintain the mission of CLOCKSS. Features such as low contribution fees for libraries and publishers, storage at multiple global locations, and open-access content available at no cost ensure safeguarding of the digital content.

As librarians and publishers continue their collaborative efforts in addressing issues regarding the preservation of electronic resources, potential obstacles such as the various e-book platforms, funding, and technological needs will diminish. Libraries have been successful in developing the means to preserve print resources. The current status of the early successful digital preservation initiatives points toward a promising tomorrow. When librarians and publishers collaborate, everyone reaps the benefits.

CONCLUSION

As librarians and vendors create innovative ways to use e-books, the e-book's significance in library collections will continue to grow. The expansion of the textbook into e-book format and the improvement of handheld devices will continue to encourage use among patrons. As patrons become familiar and more comfortable with the e-book format, use statistics will naturally increase. Use data will remain a vital part of the collection development librarian's arsenal when determining which, if any, content to purchase in e-book format. "The important thing is, when you have access to the usage data, use it! Vendors who monitor the amount of traffic in their administrative modules report that only 40 to 70 percent of libraries are actually viewing the data. Make sure you track your e-book data by assigning someone in your library to check it on a regular basis" (Polanka 2009). The COUNTER, SUSHI, and ICOLC standards will assist librarians in comparing use data among vendors. How one uses the data, whether to develop collections, to justify costs, or to track virtual library users, will vary by library and purpose. Whatever the need, as the e-book grows, the need to analyze e-book use will become more critical. Librarians would do well to take Cox's sentiment to heart: "Making sense of e-book use data is a complex process and demands persistence and flexibility on the part of librarians" (2007, 209).

Use data are useless, however, without a guarantee of perpetual access to content. Just as e-journal publishers have done, e-book publishers will need to develop plans for the preservation of e-book content for years to come. The existing CLOCKSS, LOCKSS, and Portico programs are options, but librarians and publishers must continue to work together to ensure that e-books can mesh with such systems. Innovation will prevail and, as a result, the formats and interfaces of e-books will change. The decisions made today will affect access to e-books in the future, so publishers and librarians must plan accordingly to preserve e-book content in the best possible format.

REFERENCES

Christianson, Marilyn, and Marsha Aucoin. 2005. "Electronic or Print Books: Which Are Used?" *Library Collections, Acquisitions, and Technical Services* 29 (1): 71–81.

Cox, John. 2004. "E-books: Challenges and Opportunities." *D-Lib Magazine* 10 (10): 1.

———. 2007. "Making Sense of E-book Usage Data." *Acquisitions Librarian* 19 (3/4): 193–212.

Gregory, Cynthia L. 2008. " 'But I Want a Real Book': An Investigation of Undergraduates' Usage and Attitudes toward Electronic Books." *Reference and User Services Quarterly* 47 (3): 266–273.

Grigson, Anna. 2009. "Evaluating Business Models for E-books through Usage Data Analysis: A Case Study from the University of Westminster." *Journal of Electronic Resources Librarianship* 21 (1): 62–74.

Littman, Justin, and Lynn Silipigni Connaway. 2004. "A Circulation Analysis of Print Books and E-books in an Academic Research Library." *Library Resources and Technical Services* 48 (4): 256–262.

Noorhidawati, A., and Forbes Gibb. 2008. "How Students Use E-books: Reading or Referring?" *Malaysian Journal of Library and Information Science* 13 (2): 1–14.

Polanka, Sue. 2009. "Off the Shelf: E-book Usage Data." *Booklist* 105 (15): 75.

Slater, Robert. 2009. "E-books or Print Books, 'Big Deals' or Local Selections: What Gets More Use?" *Library Collections, Acquisitions, and Technical Services* 33 (1): 31–41.

8

E-book Standards

EMILIE DELQUIÉ
AND SUE POLANKA

Currently, few standards exist for e-books, but it seems as though everyone from end users to publishers and librarians is asking for them. "Libraries are frustrated with the lack of standard practice among providers of e-books" (Anson and Connell 2009, 12). Expectations are high given all the progress made with other electronic resources in the past fifteen years, but e-books are diverse and each publisher seems to be handling them in a slightly different way. Because library wholesalers, until recently, were not prepared for e-book transactions, most e-book sales were channeled through the publisher or new aggregator platforms, a practice new and different to libraries and publishers. Moreover, publishers are willing to experiment and test different models to meet users demand. They are going to great lengths to listen to their customers and provide content in the formats that users prefer, but they are struggling to find business models beneficial to themselves, libraries, and end users. As a result, "many libraries are unprepared for the challenges in adopting, integrating, and maintaining e-books" (Anson and Connell 2009, 12). What they want are standards.

At the Charleston e-book preconference in 2009, Randy Petway of Publishing Technology characterized standards as agreements between various parties to do or say things in a particular manner (Petway 2009). If it were only that easy! The reality is that, despite the desire of librarians, users, publishers, and book vendors to have agreements or standards, they are not exactly that simple to create. Petway described a barrier to e-book standards, which he called "thirty." E-books have been around for thirty years, there are nearly thirty devices on the market (and counting), and there are thirty formats for e-book content, many of which are proprietary. An additional factor of thirty that could be added is the library factor. Librarians want standards, but the kinds and types of standards needed differ from library to library and consortium to consortium, making it challenging for publishers to meet library needs. Additionally, there are two markets working with and against one another, the academic e-book market and the trade market. Each has its own factor of thirty, which eventually need to be intertwined for some consistency in the way we purchase, read, download, print, and share our e-books. What standards are currently in place? Where should new standards begin? What standards do librarians and publishers want? What challenges prevent agreement? In this chapter we discuss these questions, addressing some existing standards and those standards or agreements that would benefit workflow in libraries.

EXISTING E-BOOK STANDARDS

EPUB

One cannot discuss e-book standards without discussing EPUB. EPUB (Electronic Publication) is an e-book standard adopted by the International Digital Publishing Forum (IDPF, www.idpf.org/specs.htm) in 2007. Its goal is to allow for the transfer of information from one device or system to another. In other words, obtaining an e-book with EPUB guarantees the ability to read the text on any portable device or computer system. EPUB is the file extension of an XML format for reflowable digital books and publications. The standard is composed of three separate open standards, the Open Publication Structure (OPS), Open Packaging Format (OPF), and Open Container Format (OCF). OPS defines the formatting of its content. OPF describes the structure of the .epub file in XML. OCF collects all files into a single file system entity.

EPUB seems to offer the beginning of a solution for standards, but the rapidly increasing offering of reader devices is bringing new questions about its consistent use. The same EPUB files can now be read differently on various readers and offer only limited flexibility with the actual design of the delivered content (Crotty 2009).

Regardless of its admitted challenges, EPUB is the most commonly adopted standard these days in an industry in much need of rules. Sony's adoption of EPUB as its standard in August 2009 should help further establish it across the industry (Herther 2009).

Supporters of EPUB cite interactivity, preservation, and ease of use for patrons and publishers as stimulants for the standard. Additionally, there is concern that the popularity of certain proprietary software will lead to a monopoly of the e-book trade market, resulting in the loss of influence or control by publishers. Supporters welcome the day when an EPUB logo will appear on e-books, announcing the freedom to read regardless of one's device (Rothman 2009).

Critics of EPUB, on the other hand, cite DRM as the primary reason EPUB will not succeed. For fear of piracy and lost revenues, nearly all publishers add DRM to e-books, even those in the EPUB format. Purchasing an e-book locked down with DRM limits its use to a particular reader or platform, thus rescinding the benefits of EPUB (Biba 2009).

Supporters and opponents aside, Michael Smith, executive director of the IDPF, said, "What is pivotal to pervasive adoption of EPUB is publisher adoption, consumer adoption, and continuous improvements and evolution of the standard" (personal communication, November 2009). The evolution of the EPUB standard is imminent. According to an IDPF press release from August 16, 2009, the EPUB standards are "open and living specifications. As a result, maintenance work involving corrections and improvements to the EPUB standard were launched, to ensure greater levels of adoption and accessibility."

XML

XML is the acronym for a widely used programming language—extensible markup language—a simple, flexible text format originally designed to meet the challenges of large-scale electronic publishing. XML helps define the book content and how that book should be formatted, allowing the file to be easily converted to meet the needs of various e-book readers, mobile devices, or websites. XML provides greater flexibility than HTML (hypertext markup language) and PDF (portable document format), and as a result many publishers use XML for e-book content, some in conjunction with the EPUB standard.

Digital Rights Management

DRM has been common practice for a long time in other media for the distribution of music, video, and audio files. It is a software technology used by publishers or other content providers to limit the use of an e-book or other electronic file. On e-books, DRM limits the way content can be used and shared. The implications of these restrictions are numerous and extremely unpopular with librarians. For example, limits imposed on printing, copying, and saving can infuriate end users and be very counter-productive. Library patrons and students in particular, who may not necessarily be able to afford a computer, find it impractical to have to read several book chapters on a library computer. Librarians are currently asking for publishers to work with them to moderate these restrictions to create an environment where they no longer hinder usage. Conversely, DRM is widely used, and accepted, in the public library market as a way to implement due dates for popular trade titles when one title is limited to one user. Publishers fear the loss of revenue and control of their digital content and thus support the use of DRM to limit the access and sharing of electronic content.

Metadata

Metadata are simply data about a digital object such as an e-book. Metadata describe an object and include bibliographic information such as author, title, publication date, and publisher as well as data about the content of the digital object and how to access it. Metadata are essential for purchasing and implementing e-books because libraries cannot discover this information when there is no print equivalent. Metadata can be loaded into a library catalog or other discovery tool, like a federated search tool, to allow patrons to search and access content. Thus, it is important that libraries ask publishers if e-book metadata are sent to link resolvers like SFX or 360 Link. Most librarians have no contact with e-book metadata until they actually reside in the library catalog in MARC record format. But for those who do work with metadata, there are several standards in place to transfer the metadata between publishers, aggregators, and libraries: METS (Metadata Encoding and Transmission Standard), EDI (Electronic Data Interchange), and TEI (Text Encoding Initiative) are popular options. ONIX (Online Information Exchange) is popular with publishers and vendors. It is an international standard containing book product data and is used to communicate these data between publishers, distributors, and other members of the bookselling industry. The ONIX metadata are broader than METS, EDI, and TEI and include promotion and territorial rights information and other things specific to the book supply chain. ONIX has not been embraced by libraries because it contains these additional data elements while lacking information specific to the MARC record such as in-depth subject headings and authorized forms of author names. Vendors who offer cataloging and metadata services to publishers have the ability to populate ONIX with metadata appropriate for the MARC record, so the distribution of ONIX records to libraries could become a practice in the future.

SERU

For an e-book to be purchased, some type of license or legal agreement must be signed between the subscribing institution and the publisher or aggregator. Due to the high cost, time commitment, and difficulty of this process, particularly for smaller libraries that may be purchasing just a few e-book titles, a recommended practice was developed to stand in place of a licensing agreement. SERU (Shared E-Resource Understanding) became a NISO-recommended practice in 2008. A NISO-recommended practice is "a best practice or guideline for methods, materials, or practices in order to give guidance to the user," where the elements are discretionary and may be used as written or modified by the users to meet specific needs (NISO 2008). SERU is not a legal document but rather a collection of statements that are agreed upon by two parties, the publisher and the subscribing institution. SERU is a risk because it is not legally binding, but it is beneficial for small purchases. SERU includes several "Statements of Common Understandings for Subscribing to Electronic Resources," which include language about subscription, the subscribing institution and its authorized users, use of materials, inappropriate use, confidentiality and privacy, online performance and service provision, and archiving and perpetual access. To implement SERU, an organization must register at the NISO SERU website (www.niso.org/committees/SERU). The statements must be mutually agreed upon by both parties. If this is not possible, then a licensing agreement must be negotiated.

International Standard Book Number

The ISBN has been around since the 1960s. It is a standard developed to facilitate a book through the supply chain. The ISBN standard, ISO 2108, requires that different product forms of a publication, if separately available, be assigned separate ISBNs (see Green 2009). So e-books and all other non-print items must have a different ISBN than their print counterpart, generally known as the e-ISBN. This practice has become increasingly problematic in recent years. The ISBN has traditionally been set by the publisher at the birth of a title. But with e-books, a publisher creates the original content file (which may get assigned an ISBN) and sends that file to multiple aggregators or distributors to convert into their proprietary formats. Because the same content has many manifestations, it is difficult for publishers to track and assign ISBNs for each version; many publishers feel the responsibility for assigning the new ISBN should fall on the aggregator or third party and as a result do not assign one. Thus, the e-book ISBN has created a multitude of problems for libraries, publishers, and end users. To assist with this problem, in April 2008 the International ISBN Agency issued a guideline that allows ISBNs to be assigned by e-book resellers, under strict conditions, when publishers do not provide their own ISBNs (see Green 2009). Unfortunately, the guideline is not ideal, and the International ISBN Agency continues to investigate ways to improve the situation; in fall 2009 it issued a survey to determine the necessary requirements (and requirements that publishers and third-party vendors would follow) for the separate identification of various e-book versions.

Digital Object Identifier

The digital object identifier (DOI) has a twofold purpose: to be a unique identifier for a known item, similar to the purpose of an ISBN, and to provide a persistent URL for the digital version of any electronic file. One of the benefits of this standard is that a book chapter, illustration, or section can have a unique DOI, linking to a much finer level of granularity than an ISBN. Many databases include DOI in the citations and as searchable fields, assisting the discovery of e-books. Like other standard numbers, the DOI has a registration agency to monitor it: R. R. Bowker and CrossRef are registration agencies in the United States.

International Standard Text Code

Adopted in 2009 as the International Standards Organization code ISO-21047, the ISTC is "a global identification system for textual works" (International ISTC Agency 2009). According to Andy Weissberg of Bowker, "The ISTC was developed to help the value chain of publishing and its various stakeholders to more effectively catalog textual works for collection development and end-user discovery, to enhance rights/royalties processing, and to enable more accurate and efficient sales analyses" (personal communication, October 2009). ISTCs will represent the text in multiple formats—print, large print, paperback, e-book, or audiobook—so long as the text is exactly the same. ISTCs are only for textual works, so books that are illustrations only are not eligible. There are three main differences between the ISTC and the ISBN. First, an ISTC represents the text (words) of an item and does not indicate a specific publisher. The ISTC is associated with the text, not with the organization. Second, ISBNs vary with format, whereas only one ISTC code is necessary to represent multiple formats. Third, the ISTC uses sixteen digits, whereas the ISBN has either eleven or thirteen. The ISTC structure is made up of four elements: registration, year, work, and check digit, as shown in table 8.1. To obtain an ISTC, one must submit metadata that uniquely describe the work to an authorized registration agency. Currently, Bowker and Nielsen are authorized agents.

STANDARD PRACTICES FAVORED BY LIBRARIES

Generally, it is fair to say that librarians expect e-book publishers to have learned from their e-journal counterparts' experiences over the past ten or fifteen years. They have already ironed out many different practicalities that result from a transition from a print to an electronic collection. They

ISTC	0A9	2009	12B4A105	7
When an ISTC is displayed it will always be preceded by the letters "ISTC"	Registration element Digits = 3 Used by the registration agency for administrative purposes	Year element Digits = 4 Represents the year in which the ISTC was registered	Work element Digits = 8 Assigned automatically by the central ISTC registration system after a metadata record has been submitted for registration and the system has verified that the record is unique	Check digit Digits = 1 Automatically generated by the ISTC registration system

TABLE 8.1 International Standard Text Code Structure

and their patrons have successfully adjusted their research and reading habits, their professional workflows, and their dealings with suppliers. As a result, they already have a strong sense of functionalities and features required for e-books to meet their needs, in terms not only of content but of the practical aspects involving e-books.

License Agreements

The availability of e-books implies that librarians need to sign a license agreement that specifically lays out the legal terms and conditions of the relationship between the publisher and the library to use the content. The core of librarians' expectations stems from their recent experience with e-journals. Currently, each publisher and aggregator suggests their own terms in their license agreements. These licenses in turn must be reviewed by librarians and in many cases their legal departments before they can proceed with any acquisition or subscription. Given that the number of publishers and available books grows all the time, this added time-consuming task can be worrisome for institutions of any size. In addition, some libraries have to sign a new license agreement with a service provider for their e-book collections even though they already have an agreement in place for their e-journals.

To avoid duplication of time and resources, librarians would like to have the option of a standard license agreement, adaptable enough to fit the different publishers' business models and the varied institutions' setups. SERU is an option, but it still requires libraries to sign the agreement with each publisher or vendor independently and presents a level of risk for both parties since the document is not binding.

From a publisher's standpoint, complying with fair-competition laws around the globe makes one unique license agreement across the industry impossible. Given that publishing houses operate from a variety of countries and that their customers are truly global, it is clear that a single legal document cannot fit all situations. Moreover, the basic antitrust laws make it simply illegal for competitors to discuss their business models (Cox 2009). Nevertheless, as publishers refine their terms with experience and librarians' feedback, one can expect some level of standardization—or at least consistency—for the topics discussed below.

Perpetual Access

Perpetual access is a major cause of concern for any librarian, especially during the transition from print to electronic books. Up until now, a library could buy a book and own it forever, assuming it was properly protected and conserved. For e-books, however, the concept of long-term ownership is currently not systematically offered by publishers, leaving libraries the choice between losing access to content they paid for once or paying a fee for as long as they wish to maintain their access. Neither option is economically viable in the long term, nor do they ensure against something happening to the publisher who owns the rights to a book.

The past decade has seen the emergence of important initiatives such as LOCKSS, CLOCKSS, and Portico for other electronic resources (see chapter 7). E-book publishers are slowly starting to incorporate these long-term preservation strategies into their planning. On the one hand, librarians expect involvement in such initiatives and find them to be attractive selling points for any content. On the other hand, publishers have understood the need to offer this type of guarantee.

Still, some contractual and technical complications that were not an issue with electronic journals need to be taken into consideration by e-book publishers. For example, as Heather Ruland Staines of Springer points out,

"Book contracts often contain a provision that requires copyright to revert to the author in the event of a publisher bankruptcy or other development that renders the book unavailable to the market place" (Ruland Staines 2009). This type of clause can be adjusted moving forward but does create some added scrutiny for all existing contracts. In the end, e-books preservation is being addressed by librarians and publishers together, but it does still require more fine-tuning before it can be a systematic practice.

Concurrent Use

Concurrent use policy also has librarians questioning the rationale behind existing DRM restrictions. Up until a few years ago, a book could be used only by one person at a time once it was checked out. Now, online platforms offer great possibilities to ensure that the expense associated with a book purchase benefits far more students and that research reaches a larger audience. Unfortunately, unlimited or reasonably limited concurrent use is not common practice for e-books, leaving librarians little flexibility and forcing them to explain to their confused patrons why they cannot consult a book online right now.

Publishers are currently experimenting with different models, and even though some of their options are attractive they also tend to be pricey. They need to protect their revenue stream and contracts they have established with their own authors, but offering content on an electronic platform now allows for flexible pricing models in the short term. For example, if an e-book is not available in the library at a certain point, an individual may have the option of renting it for a week, or a faculty member may be able to access it for the length of the term.

Interlibrary Loan and Course Reserve

Along the same lines as concurrent use for a print book, libraries would like to continue to lend their books to other institutions and not be restricted by DRM. Students have come to rely on ILL to supplement their research in areas where their libraries may have limited funds to expand their collections. As it stands now, once a library purchases an e-book, it loses the option of sharing that e-book with other libraries. This is a critical service to many libraries, particularly those involved in consortia, public libraries with multiple branches, and multiple schools within a district. Moreover, few publishers or aggregators are equipped to sell single-title e-books to consortia, which would replace the need for ILL within a larger group. In a survey conducted in 2007 by ebrary to over five hundred librarians around the world, a majority of respondents (59 percent) were somewhat to very concerned about ILL in the context of e-books (ebrary 2007). In spite of this and the growing concern expressed by librarians, few changes have been implemented in the license agreements currently used.

Librarians also want to be able to put some of their e-books, or at least some chapters, on reserve as needed by faculty. There is growing interest among academic libraries to purchase book chapters rather than entire e-books and to organize these chapters into course materials. EBL, an e-book aggregator, currently offers this service. But most publishers are hesitant to give libraries more flexibility when it comes to ILL and electronic reserve, often because they are concerned about the repercussions on their ability to sell more copies. Transferring the electronic version of a book is a much simpler process than sending a physical copy by mail, despite the general perception that it is otherwise. Although some publishers have understood the importance of this requirement, it appears that others are still struggling to find the right fee for this benefit. Finding the right fee also requires libraries to pay that fee, a situation that is usually met with resistance.

Use Statistics

Use statistics are one of the key elements of the evaluation of any resource for most collections. Librarians rely on them heavily when deciding which resources to renew or to cancel every year. This assumes, though, that the data they have allow them to compare the resources they are evaluating fairly. Aside from the reality that different types of resources have different use levels in each subject area, it is key to know that the supplied numbers can indeed be compared because they derive from some sort of standard. Specifically, the number of clicks, page views, chapter or abstract views, or search requests can vary greatly by and within a platform, and each brings a whole different context for those statistics. The minimal standard applicable for e-books would be one similar to the COUNTER-compliant statistics used for e-journals. Use statistics are discussed in greater depth in chapter 7.

Software Discrepancies

The various e-book providers currently have different sets of rules when it comes to the delivery of their content. For instance, some platforms let users access content on their site, whereas others require users to install or use proprietary software. Providers who maintain their own e-book readers add another dimension, since content may be device specific. Aside from the lack of consistency, this also creates some internal and technical difficulties for libraries. Can the proprietary software be installed on any computer a patron wishes to use? Can the library offer only a particular title or collection on specific stations? Can one reserve computer time at this particular machine for this designated purpose? What happens when the software needs to be updated on all computers on which it is installed? If a library wants to offer content on e-book readers, which readers are compatible with the titles the library has already purchased?

This situation can also be confusing for the end user, who may not realize that certain content is unavailable until the software is downloaded. Finally, each new platform and software application requires a learning curve, which slows down research, which in turn reduces the usage of those resources. "The lack in technological development standards has resulted in libraries having to maintain multiple formats, hardware and software" (Jenkins 2008). Ideally, every chapter and page could be accessed in PDF or XML from the publishers' platform and would not require any additional downloads. At this point, publishers are still experimenting to find their competitive advantage and are increasingly responsive to these software concerns. The adoption of standards such as EPUB and the popularization of e-books by the general public should help these concerns fade away in the near future.

Printing and Downloading

As much as patrons enjoy conducting their research online, they also have limited tolerance for reading pages on a computer screen. They may also have limited time to spend at one location and may wish to print or take a chapter with them. The current DRM restrictions often prevent or significantly limit the options for printing from an e-book. These restrictions certainly have sound practical and economic reasons behind them, but they also impact the attractiveness of using content from e-books. Librarians would prefer to set those limits themselves, being well aware of the fair-use clauses included in the license agreements they sign.

DRM can also limit functions as simple as cutting and pasting a paragraph, or saving a copy of a PDF to a separate drive. The impossibility of using these basic functions also detracts from the practicality of e-books for patrons, who sometimes simply do not have time to read a whole chapter or book at once. They might also need to refer to the material later in their research and cannot always afford to go back to the library to consult the reference or paragraph they found, nor do they want to replicate steps in their research process.

Today, most publishers resist lifting DRM restrictions, but as more and more innovators lead the way and can show that a DRM-free environment does not threaten their bottom line, improvements can be expected to follow.

Delays in Publication and Access

In spite of all the technological progress made in the past twenty years, e-books are often not released until after their print counterpart. This lag of time between the two formats influences librarians' selection processes and creates justified frustration. A survey of ARL libraries in 2009 indicated that e-book purchases would increase if those titles were available at the same time as the print version (Anson and Connell 2009, 21). Similarly, electronic access is not consistently activated right after an order is placed by the library. Thus, it becomes increasingly challenging to track when an e-book can actually be added to a collection and used by patrons. Various publishers activate access as the order is received, as the invoice is paid, or at some point during (or after) the process. These delays can be avoided by streamlining operations and offering better communication between publishers and librarians. Librarians and patrons have to rely on and expect quick access to resources online and certainly hope that these problems are only part of this transition period.

Pricing Models

Existing pricing models lack consistency and offer limited flexibility to libraries. For the most part, e-books can be purchased or subscribed to as single titles; bundled in a preset collection by subject area, publisher, or both on an aggregator's platform; or purchased or leased on a pay-per-view model. Although each model has its advantages and disadvantages, librarians typically have little room to negotiate pricing structures with publishers given the current lack of flexibility and limited concurrent use. Practically speaking, pricing models cannot be standardized for obvious competitive reasons. Furthermore, nonstandardized pricing creates a healthy environment for innovation and flexibility.

Some publishers are currently experimenting with new models based on FTEs, (full-time equivalents) or sometimes on proportional FTEs; for example, a four-year school might receive a price for 100 percent of its FTEs, whereas a public library is quoted for some percentage of its geographic or user population. As mentioned above, some books are simply available for rent for a short period or by pay-per-view at the chapter level. Pricing models for e-books no longer need to be based on an annual subscription, thereby creating new opportunities for publishers to offer competitive and original structures.

Another increasingly popular model is the open-access e-book, which can avoid all the DRM restrictions. But this model raises a different set of questions related to maintaining quality and peer review standards. In the end, libraries have limited funds and want flexible pricing models that reflect their unique situations, whether their institution is a small college, one of a multisite campus or district, or a stand-alone special library.

MARC Records and Linking Capabilities

Librarians eagerly await more standardization from publishers for the metadata they provide. Specifically, e-books introduce new workflows for librarians and can include the addition of hundreds of MARC records in a short period of time. Currently, some e-book providers offer the inclusion of these MARC records as part as their service or for an additional fee, but the quality of these records is often inconsistent and they may be unusable in a library catalog. Although it is commonly understood that it is not simple for publishers to provide records that are exactly in line with OCLC standards, a minimum level of consistency and accuracy seems mandatory if the service is to be advertised—or offered at an additional fee. MARC records should be in a format that is easy to import and requires as little additional manual updating as possible.

At the same time, the metadata provided by publishers should allow for easy linking and integration in the library's OPAC, federated searching, and link resolvers. Libraries expect from e-book providers both catalog data for formal cataloging (e.g., author, year, source, size) and elements that define the contents, such as keywords or controlled vocabulary (Ball 2009). The basic MARC record information should include subject headings that accurately reflect content, a capacity to locate items via faceted search engines and browsing, and URLs/DOIs that work consistently (Rupp-Serrano 2008). Some have suggested the broad adoption of the MARC Record Guide for Monograph Aggregator Vendors. Publishers are debating the viability of this level of involvement. Although they see the competitive advantage in offering it, many have started to realize their shortcomings in this area. They also need to evaluate their investment when, in the long run, the MARC record they create is being used and transferred in platforms to benefit other companies. Collaboration between librarians and vendors is currently under way to establish whose responsibility this standard—or service—falls under, and a consensus should also be reached in the short term. Additionally, vendors offer contract cataloging services to publishers that include the complete MARC record for e-book titles. Though a great service, this can be a significant expense to publishers, who need to justify the extra investment in their e-book prices.

CONCLUSION

Although e-book standards have much room for growth and improvement today, publishers and librarians can be commended for their recent, ongoing dialog and for the time they have all invested to implement rapid improvements in the past few years. It is true that the mistakes made when journals shifted from print to electronic format provide concrete examples of what does and does not work, but all the parties involved in this supply chain have been particularly open to embracing this change.

Furthermore, it is important to keep in mind that e-books are still in an early stage of their cycle and that the lack of standardization has probably led to much innovation that benefits the industry. An e-book no longer has to be considered as a whole entity but can be identified at a much more granular level. Publishers, librarians, and end users have an opportunity to rethink the way the information is searched, packaged, delivered, sold, and read.

In the next few years it is fair to expect much improvement in the way e-books are delivered, introduced, and hosted as organizations continue to strive to establish some standards. At the same time, while there is a lot of activity in the academic and library markets, the consumer market and large players in the trade book industry are driving innovation in parallel. The two segments' needs differ somewhat, but the general public's adoption should help decision makers finalize standards more rapidly.

Finally, as new e-book technologies continue to be introduced, all the players involved will need to keep the dialog open in hope of developing standards that address and optimize the basic needs. It is clear that e-book standards have much room for growth and improvement. The twenty-first-century challenge is to connect the dots of publishers, libraries, online vendors, and device manufacturers to draw a standard picture.

REFERENCES

Anson, C., and R. R. Connell. 2009. *SPEC Kit 313: E-book Collections.* Washington, D.C.: Association of Research Libraries.

Ball, Rafael. 2009. "E-books in Practice: The Librarian's Perspective." *Learned Publishing* 21 (1): 18–22, http://epub.uni-regensburg.de/2047/1/Ball.pdf.

Biba, Paul. 2009. "EPUB Is Irrelevant to the Consumer; DRM Is the Issue; Amazon Is Brilliant." Tate Publishing, May 6, www.teleread .org/2009/05/06/epub-is-irrelevant-to-the-consumer-drm-is-the-issue-amazon-is-brilliant/.

Cox, John. 2009. "Developing an E-book Business Model: Too New for Standardization?" Presentation to the Book Industry Study Group, American Library Association, 2009, www.slideshare.net/bisg/ala2009john-cox-john -cox-associates.

Crotty, David. 2009. "New Technologies and the Need for Standards." *The Scholarly Kitchen,* September 10, http://scholarlykitchen.sspnet .org/2009/09/10/new-technologies-and-the-need-for-standards/.

ebrary. 2007. *ebrary's Global eBook Survey.* Palo Alto, Calif., www.ebrary.com/ corp/collateral/en/Survey/ebrary_eBook_survey_2007.pdf.

Green, Brian. 2009. "E-books and ISBNs: Requirements for Separate Identification of Different E-book Versions." www.jiscebooksproject.org/ wp-content/091123-isbn-ebook-requirements.doc.

Herther, Nancy. 2009. "Sony Announces New Ebook Readers and EPUB Standard Support." Information Today, August 20, http://newsbreaks.infotoday.com/ NewsBreaks/Sony-Announces-New-Ebook-Readers-and-EPUB-Standard -Support-55729.asp.

International ISTC Agency. 2009. "All about ISTC." www.istc-international.org/ index.php?ci_id = 1817.

Jenkins, Alanna. 2008. "What Is Inhibiting the Proliferation of E-books in the Academic Library?" *Scroll* 1 (1), https://jps.library.utoronto.ca/index.php/ fdt/article/viewArticle/4905/1764.

NISO. 2008. *SERU: A Shared Electronic Resource Understanding.* NISO RP-7-2008. NISO, www.niso.org/workrooms/seru.

Petway, Randy. 2009. "Ebook Standards." Presentation by author. 29th Annual Charleston Conference, 2009, www.libraries.wright.edu/noshelfrequired/ wp-content/uploads/2009/11/petway.pdf.

Rothman, David. 2009. "Epub? Plenty of Point to It. Cross-platform DRM? Pointless. Amazon Biz Approach? Dangerous to Consumers." www.teleread .org/2009/05/07/epub-plenty-of-point-to-it-cross-platform-drm-pointless -amazon-biz-approach-dangerous/.

Ruland Staines, Heather. 2009. "Springer's eBook Preservation Strategy." *Against the Grain* 21 (1): 28–32.

Rupp-Serrano, Karen. 2008. "Electronic Resources and Libraries." https:// smartech.gatech.edu/bitstream/1853/20768/5/shooting-fish.ppt.

9

The Future of Academic Book Publishing: E-books and Beyond

ROLF JANKE

For more than one hundred years, academic book publishers have remained sheltered from any prolific change that would turn their business upside down, until now. With increasingly higher demands for online content, it is no surprise that e-books will play a large role in changing what was once one of the most traditional of industries. The race is on among vendors and publishers to take advantage of this rapidly growing new marketplace. The advances in technology that allow e-books to go mobile, to be downloaded, customized, or sent instantly across the globe change daily, and the economically strapped publishing industry built primarily for a printed book environment has to change as well. How individuals access digital content will depend largely on how academic publishers adapt to the new digital environment.

Publishers have embraced the e-book as a new product model but still have a great deal to absorb in order for it to be a sustainable component of their business. Absorbing the rapid changes in e-book technology alone seems like an insurmountable task. Technology is not the only challenge, though, as publishers are changing their traditional editorial and production processes to become more efficient at publishing and distributing digital content. It is fascinating to think that, for decades, academic publishers were entrenched in a print world, and now the emergence of e-books has totally turned this world upside down overnight. But change is inevitable, as Sue Polanka notes: "Change is constant and provides opportunities and threats at every corner" (Polanka 2009).

Where are publishers now with the realization that e-books are here to stay? What challenges and opportunities do they have? How can they assist the library community to make their content more discoverable? What will happen to print? In this chapter I explore what academic publishers have learned so far about e-books and what their plans are to remain competitive in a constantly changing market.

PRINT: SAFETY IN NUMBERS

Before looking into the future of e-books from a publisher's perspective, one must consider the foundation that most publishers built before they even thought about publishing or launching an e-book. Since the beginning, academic publishers of reference works, textbooks, and monographs had one goal in mind for a book: develop it, produce it, and get it to the customer. This might seem like an overly simple process, but it is quite an involving ordeal that publishers always try to perfect, to keep cost effective, and, for all, to make profitable. It is important to understand this traditional process in order to understand why publishers are where they are today and why it is still not a perfect world for them.

In the print world, publishers created editorial models that allowed them to build publishing programs that would brand them as specialists in one or more disciplines. These models set them up for the specific types of products they would create, such as reference works, monographs, or textbooks. The editorial process was the core function, and this still holds true whether a company is publishing print or electronic products. But many publishers that built their editorial process on the foundation that the content would be bound and printed soon learned that with e-books a whole new set of challenges would appear.

One such challenge was content conversion, the process of converting word files into coded files such as XML that allow the content to maintain the greatest flexibility on an e-book platform. Another challenge was the perplexing rights management issue; electronic rights were needed even when one had secured print rights. Probably the biggest challenge was deciding how many books to print with the knowledge that an electronic version's sales could displace print sales. Before e-books emerged, for example, a typical print run on an encyclopedia for the life of the edition was two thousand units. But now, publishers are printing encyclopedias as well as offering them as e-books. How might this affect a print run? It differs between publishers, but it is highly unlikely that a publisher prints two thousand units, and in some cases the run may even be lower than half of that. Of course, economic conditions play a large role in potential sales of a product, but the bottom line is that shrinking print runs are a result of e-books replacing print sales.

Looking at the economics of this more closely, it is not entirely a dire situation to have an increase of e-books and a decrease of print books, but the publisher must weigh what the minimum print run could be to sustain a reasonable profit margin because lower runs mean higher unit costs. Higher unit costs could eventually mean that a print publishing program is no longer sustainable, or that a publisher no longer has the required financial resources to allocate to book publishing. These reasons are why there are still so many print books available during a time when e-books may be preferable. Thus, the publishers must adapt—but how?

THE PARADIGM SHIFT:
THE PRINTED WORD GOES DIGITAL

For publishers, moving into the digital realm has been an arduous task, and the main challenge is investing in technology. Before a publisher even can launch an e-book, it must decide how it will disseminate the content digitally. The most common options are to self-host on a platform the publisher invests in a vendor to build or, to avoid that costly process, to simply license the content to an e-book aggregator. These options are discussed in more detail below.

Few, if any, book publishers have the experience or the systems to build an e-book platform internally. Thus, the alternative is to seek out a technology vendor who can best equip them with a customized platform. The type of content one produces can dictate the scope of the platform built, but the advantages of a customized platform can help the publisher maintain its brand and commitment to the quality behind the content. For example, a journals publisher might seek different functionality on a platform than a monograph publisher.

Investing in such a platform is expensive, and it is a cost publishers have not had to deal with until recently. Still, most major academic publishers have built, via a technology vendor, their own e-book platforms and created their own pricing and access and hosting models to go with them. The ability of a publisher to host its own content has become popular due to the controls the publisher can place on what products are put online, how much to charge for the products, and, if updates are required, the ability to add them as needed. This flexibility has allowed publishers to create savvy e-book platforms, but the market quickly became flooded with them. This result created a myriad of pricing and access models that the customer had to choose from, ranging from perpetual ownership to a subscription model. The solution that most librarians currently desire is a reasonable one: buy and host all their content on one standard platform. It is unlikely that publishers will band together to have their content hosted on one standard platform, so they are now more willing to license their content to e-book aggregators, which in many ways can serve as a standard platform with consistent pricing. Even though publishers continue to invest in their own platforms, licensing content to aggregators such as NetLibrary, Gale Virtual Reference Library, ebrary, and Credo Reference has become a necessary component of their overall e-book strategy.

There are, however, pros and cons to licensing content to e-book aggregators. On the positive side, aggregators have the expertise in technology and content delivery that allows a seamless process for publishers to offer their content online, especially if they do not have their own e-book platform. Aggregators are usually more adaptive to new technological trends or applications which, in many ways, make their delivery system more state of the art than that of a publisher. On the negative side, each aggregator has its own business model and content conversion requirements. Taking the content conversion requirement into consideration can be a costly choice for a publisher. Certain aggregators require publishers to submit XML files rather than PDF files. If the publisher does not have the required file format, it is charged for the conversion. Included in each aggregator's business model is its own licensing arrangement with publishers. A publisher can license a book to aggregator A and the same book to aggregator B and receive two entirely different financial arrangements. Assuming the financial arrangements regardless of the aggregator are acceptable, it is difficult to predict how many titles will be sold on a regular basis, so forecasting licensing revenue is challenging.

A final disadvantage of e-book aggregators is the weakening of publisher brand identity. Publishers value their brand, and many customers become loyal to certain publishing brands. The bottom line for aggregators is to acquire as much content as possible, because the more content they have, the more money they make. A publisher that adds one hundred titles to an e-book vendor that already has five thousand titles in its system from hundreds of publishers finds it difficult to maintain any brand identity. This problem slightly goes against the publisher's mantra of valuing the content it publishes.

E-BOOKS AND ECONOMICS

The economics of e-books have changed the financial mind-set of publishers and how they approach retaining, if not increasing, their bottom line expectations. Print sales, especially, are declining. As mentioned earlier, there are new expense considerations that come with e-books, such as conversion costs and higher print unit costs, but e-books also present some efficiencies. Publishers are taking advantage of these efficiencies.

Distribution is far more cost effective for e-books than print books because there are no fulfillment, inventory, and shipping costs. Publishers who ship hundreds or thousands of books per day see huge savings if they fulfill an e-book order rather than a bound book order. There are no returns on e-books, which solves an age-old problem publishers faced as monthly returns from library wholesalers appeared. The cost of processing returns disappears too, and the revenue reports look a lot better without a credit column added to them. Discounts given to library wholesalers may become more moderate since the wholesalers do not handle, ship, or process physical inventory. Wholesalers have become active in e-book transactions between libraries and publishers, and the discount rates set for e-books are proportionately lower than for bound books.

Publishers are taking advantage of these cost savings and have even begun to create born-digital e-books. Even though there may be a slim print market for a particular book type, such as monographs, publishers bypass the print run altogether to save costs by offering only a digital version. If the library wants a print edition, there are efficient and cost-effective print-on-demand options available to them, such as Ingram's Lightning Source. Publishers make their files available to these vendors so they can keep their print-buying customers happy while maintaining a reasonable profit margin by selling the digital version. With these cost efficiencies in mind, publishers have found ways to offset the costs which, as mentioned earlier, challenged them as they created their e-book strategy.

Once a publisher has established its e-book strategy, new revenue opportunities are created out of a successful e-book program. Publishers can sell e-books in collections and offer a discount to libraries based on a bulk purchase. Reference and monograph collections are popular and will grow even more popular as libraries run out of shelf space. For example, libraries can now buy an entire reference collection without taking up any more room. Collections are also a must for publishers, because libraries continue to demand more and more from consortia, and consortia traditionally do not offer their member institutions single e-book purchasing.

Though still untested and unproven, there are two new opportunists for publishers to sell their e-book content: pay-per-view and buy-by-the-chapter or by-the-article. Pay-per-view is potentially the riskier of the two options for book content, as far as publishers are concerned. Pay-per-view is available now with journals, but customers may question the value of that type of content over that of an encyclopedia. Will a customer pay $0.99 just to view a 1,500-word article? Publishers doubt that they will and are thus far more intrigued about selling their content in chunks.

The Article Economy

The pay-per-view model has opened new markets that journal publishers have discovered since offering their content online—that is, a potentially robust market exists for selling individual journal articles. By selling journal articles individually, journal publishers vastly increase their customer reach to those who are not interested in subscribing to annual journals but are interested in one article. The same can be applied to publishers of e-books. Academic publishers of edited works such as handbooks and encyclopedias are now considering selling chapters and entries. If they sell an article on a purchase model, the revenue incurred on that item would be incremental. This means that a significant amount of volume would have to be sold to make it a profitable venture.

The real proof that this model might work lies in the popularity of smartphones, such as the iPhone. Several publishers are considering adding an application to the iPhone service that enables their content to be discovered at the article level. This is a fascinating prospect for publishers who perhaps can create new e-book products, specifically for these phones, that might go beyond just one article. A small chunk of related content that could be updated or revised could then be sold via a subscription model, which would allow customers to have continual access to the content they want, when they want it, and at an affordable price.

The Free Economy

"Is free the future?" This is the lead question in a *New Yorker* magazine article by Malcolm Gladwell titled "Priced to Sell" (2009). The Web is a virtual playground of free information, but, when it comes to the future of academic content in the digital realm, will it ever all be offered for free? That outcome is highly unlikely, but the concept of free information seems inevitable. In his article, Gladwell endorses this notion through a savvy review of *Free: The Future of a Radical Price,* by Chris Anderson (2009). This book is certainly not the first to describe the notion that information wants to be free. For publishers, the concept of "free information" has been challenging. Publishers are in the business of developing and disseminating content (or in this case, information), and in the academic publishing business this information is written from an authoritative perspective. Thus, publishers charge for the content. In the era of Wikipedia, the same type of information may exist, and for free—but is it authoritative? If a student doing research for a term paper needs information fast, what source will she chose? The notion of "free" can easily impact her decision. Wikipedia is a useful resource, but like all free information found on the Web it has its limitations. Publishers must accept that free information is a fact of the current and future information environment, but they can still maintain a sustainable business by providing authoritative content via new digital content delivery models.

E-BOOK READERS

As the choice to access free or paid content online becomes more desirable, the ways in which one can have it delivered are growing. As e-books were evolving, there were still only limited ways to make the content available. One could access the content on a computer that perhaps was networked into a system where the purchased e-books were stored. This is the basic model in the library setting where e-books are subscribed to or purchased from a publisher or aggregator.

Just as publishers became more adaptive in pricing and servicing this model, the introduction of an obvious technological solution to e-book viewing hit the market by storm. E-readers emerged on the scene only a few short years ago. In 2007, Amazon released the first-generation Kindle, a handheld reading device that stores e-books. Amazon even has an online bookstore to go with it. Although there was a hefty cost to the Kindle at $359, the cost of an e-book for the device was high. "In the digital books world, a number of the costs are removed, so we believe [e-books] should be priced lower," said Russell Grandinetti, vice president of books for Amazon (Grossman and Sachs 2009, 102). The price of $9.95 for down-loading an e-book to a handheld device was an instant wake-up call for publishers.

The e-reader phenomenon as it relates to academic publishing is another issue altogether. Reading a novel on a reader is an unusual expe-rience, but novels probably fit the technology more than other types of books. For the college textbook market, Amazon created a version of the Kindle 2, the DX, which was launched to promote easier viewing of text-books and periodicals. Many textbooks have complex tables and graphics, and though the larger DX screen can accommodate those, they still lack color.

The lack of color is not the only thing that seems to be turning col-lege students away from the Kindle DX. In a pilot program at Princeton

University, fifty students received the DX at no cost. But according to the *Daily Princetonian,* the students' experiences were not encouraging for the Kindle: "Much of my learning comes from a physical interaction with the text: bookmarks, highlights, page-tearing . . . not to mention margin notes . . . all these things have been lost," stated one student (Lee 2009). One might assume such a reaction to any device that attempts to display a textbook, not just the Kindle.

Aside from textbooks, other products on e-readers may have better odds with students. Academic journal and reference publishers are looking carefully at the business models and prospects of allowing their content to be sold through the reader channel. A small chunk of information, such as a journal article, might be a more palatable sale to a student or researcher than a full textbook. The idea appears viable, but publishers also question how many end users of their content own an e-reader. Publishers also wonder what type of device most students own, and could that device easily store and display a short article? For example, smartphones are becoming more advanced and even more affordable, especially to college students. Publishers are more than aware of this, and it seems there is a more positive reaction to disseminating content through smartphone technology than through e-readers. It is doubtful that a student would want an organic biology text on his smartphone, but from an economic standpoint publishers might sustain a decent return on their investment by selling an encyclopedia article or journal article as a onetime purchase using the smartphone service for distribution.

CHALLENGES MOVING FORWARD: PACE VERSUS OUTCOMES

The challenges that e-books pose to publishers go way beyond studying the economics, reengineering the editorial process, and adapting to new distribution models. If publishers satisfactorily figure out those three components alone, they will have won only half the battle. On the other side of this battle are several challenges still to be faced.

The important concept of discoverability is a serious one that has been debated among publishers and libraries. The creation of an acceptable standard that all parties can agree on is necessary. The technology is there, but publishers often find themselves wondering if there is a more affordable solution that does not require a huge investment. Partnering with vendors such as Serials Solutions and its KnowledgeWorks, which contains over two million e-books and journal holdings from hundreds of publishers, might seem like an affordable solution. Simply licensing content onto as many e-book aggregators as possible could be another remedy.

The outcome of using such services might make the content discoverable, but how does such a relationship protect the publisher's brand? Would the end users even care who the publisher is behind the content? Probably not. Publishers must decide what the overall impact of the discoverability revolution to their business will be. They all believe in their brand and the importance of enhancing it, but marketing that brand becomes difficult if their content is just a tiny portion of a much larger resource.

The pace of technology will also have a tremendous impact on e-book publishers. Smartphones are popular now, but what will be next? While publishers are figuring out the business model for the current technology, a new device or process will be introduced and new models will have to be considered. Publishers are driven by producing high-quality content and getting it to the customer, which are part of their conservative and traditional core values. Trying to stay ahead or even on top of the technology curve is virtually impossible for a publisher, and it is perhaps for this reason that companies such as Amazon and Google have taken a leading role in the content distribution business. They are not just keeping pace, they are setting the pace.

The aggressive pace to provide more e-books has serious implications for print. There are cost implications for reducing print runs, but those can be managed provided that the publisher effectively replaces print revenue with revenue from electronic products. But there is a larger issue to consider: is print dead in the academic library?

The immediate answer is no, or perhaps not yet. Declining print sales for reference and monograph works are expected year on year to the point that publishers may have to consider making their book strategies solely born digital. It is difficult to predict when and if this will happen on a global scale, but as the demand for e-books and other electronic content increases, publishers will have to phase out specific processes that are tied to producing print just to stay profitable. This may sound like an extreme scenario, but even though publishers might not keep the proper pace with all of the elements, they still believe in the great opportunities e-books can create for them, and the outcomes will be maximized.

REFERENCES

Anderson, Chris. 2009. *Free: The Future of a Radical Price.* New York: Hyperion.

Gladwell, Malcolm. 2009. "Priced to Sell." *New Yorker,* July.

Grossman, Lev, and Andrea Sachs. 2009. "Big River." *Time,* June, 101–103.

Lee, Hyung. 2009. "Kindles Yet to Woo University Users." *Daily Princetonian,* November 16, www.dailyprincetonian.com/2009/09/28/23918/.

Polanka, Sue. 2009. "Introduction." *Journal of Library Administration* 49 (May/ June 2009): 325–326.

CONTRIBUTORS

ANNE BEHLER is an information literacy librarian at the Penn State University Libraries, focused on instruction and outreach to first-year students. She is also the librarian for the Penn State University Park leisure reading collection and is co–project leader for the Penn State Sony Reader pilot project. Her research interests include literacy among higher-education students and outreach and marketing to first-year students.

SUSAN BERG has extensive experience as a school librarian and technology supervisor working in urban and suburban school districts. She has an AMLS from the University of Michigan and a PhD in educational leadership from the University of Dayton. Currently she is the school library media program advisor at Wright State University.

SHONDA BRISCO is an assistant professor and the curriculum materials librarian at Oklahoma State University in Stillwater, where she works with preservice teachers in the College of Education. Shonda has a BA in English and journalism and an MLIS. She currently writes the Digital Resources column for *School Library Journal* and is pursuing her PhD in educational technology.

JACKIE COLLIER is an associate professor in the College of Education Human Services/Teacher Education Department at Wright State University. Her current roles include coordinator of the Reading Endorsement and Reading Masters programs and site coordinator of Reading Recovery at Wright State. Jackie's areas of interest include reading and writing pedagogy in schools and differentiated curriculum to meet the needs of diverse learners. Her PhD, earned in 1996 from Miami University of Ohio, is in educational learnership: curriculum development. Since joining Wright State, she has become involved in bringing online instruction to the department. In 1994 she was Ohio's Teacher of the Year.

ALICE CROSETTO has been an educator and librarian at both the high school and university levels in the Cleveland and Youngstown, Ohio, areas for more than thirty years. From Kent State University, Ohio, she has earned a BA in Latin, MA in English, MEd in curriculum and instruction, and MLS. She has been at the University Libraries, University of Toledo, since 2005 as the coordinator for collection development and the acquisitions librarian. Alice has published articles and presented in the area of collection development and literature awards for children. In addition, she writes book reviews for *American Reference Books Annual* and has several entries in Bowker's *RCL: Resources for College Libraries* and *RCL: Career Resources.* Her first book, *Disabilities and Disorders in Literature for Youth: A Selective Annotated Bibliography for K-12,* was published September 2009.

EMILIE DELQUIÉ has been an active member of the information industry for over nine years. After working for five years with the collection development team in an academic library and earning a BS in marketing from the University of Massachusetts in Boston, she is now responsible for all aspects of Publishers Communication Group's research services. In this role, she analyzes results from market research campaigns and online surveys to advise publishers on their sales and marketing strategies. Recently, she has conducted studies on librarians' attitudes toward e-books, in order to help publishers develop offerings that meet libraries' needs.

BLAISE DIERKS is the head of adult services at the River Forest Public Library, Illinois. Blaise received her MLIS from Dominican University in 2006 and has been at the River Forest Public Library since 2005.

JAMES GALBRAITH is the associate director for collections and scholarly resources at DePaul University in Chicago. Previously, he has been assistant director for collections for Columbia University, head of collections at Wake Forest University, and head of collections at the University of California, Irvine. Jim has written about business information resources, GIS, music, and most recently Google News.

He has an MA in history from the University of Illinois at Urbana-Champaign and an MLS from SUNY Buffalo.

ROLF JANKE, founder and vice president/publisher for Sage Reference, has been involved in academic publishing for more than twenty-eight years, with experience in text, trade, academic, and reference publishing. At Sage he is responsible for the strategic development and growth of a reference product line directed toward academic and public libraries. He has spoken at many conferences on the future of electronic reference and is a member of the American Library Association. Prior to Sage, Rolf was vice president and publisher for ABC-CLIO and editorial director for Blackwell Publishers. He started his career in sales and editorial at Kent Publishing, a division of International Thomson.

CAROLYN MORRIS graduated from Middlebury College with a BA in history. She began working in academic book supply as publisher relations specialist for YBP Library Services in 2000. She is currently director of U.S. Sales for Coutts Information Services, an Ingram Content Company.

AMY PAWLOWSKI, currently the web applications manager at the Cleveland Public Library, manages the development, implementation, and maintenance of web-based library services for the library and the CLEVNET consortium. Amy has held several positions in the library field, including manager of partner services for OverDrive, where she assisted libraries with training, marketing, outreach, and collection development for their digital library platform. She has also worked as archivist for the Cleveland Orchestra, technology and information literacy librarian at Cuyahoga Community College, and public services coordinator for the Hartt School of Performing Arts Library at the University of Hartford.

LINDSEY SCHELL is the bibliographer for journals, English literature, and gender studies at the University of Texas Libraries in Austin, where she has worked for ten years. She received her MLS from the University of North Carolina at Chapel Hill and a BA from Tufts University in history and women's studies. She serves on the collections team, manages budgets and policies related to serials in all disciplines, and coordinates pay-per-view pilot programs. She has written and presented about e-books in national and international forums since 2002.

LISA SIBERT, electronic resources acquisitions librarian at the University of California, Irvine, manages the life cycle of digital resources across all academic fields served by UCI Libraries. She is involved in local pilot projects designed to build UCI Libraries' e-book collection and in customizing the local electronic records management system to manage the growing number of e-books acquired by UCI. Lisa has spoken about electronic resources and e-books at several professional conferences, including Electronic Resources and Libraries, North American Serials Interest Group, and the Charleston Conference. She has an MLIS from the University of Illinois at Urbana-Champaign and a BA in comparative literature from California State University, Long Beach.

INDEX

You may also be interested in

Fundamentals of Collection Development and Management, Second Edition. Peggy Johnson offers a comprehensive tour of this essential discipline and situates the fundamental ideas of collection development and management in historical and theoretical perspective, bringing this modern classic fully up to date.

Developing an Outstanding Core Collection: A Guide for Libraries, Second Edition. In this practical handbook, Carol Alabaster focuses on developing a collection with high-quality materials while saving time and money. Packed with selection resources and sample core lists in seven subject areas, this soup-to-nuts manual will be useful whether you are starting from scratch or revitalizing an existing collection.

The Readers' Advisory Handbook. Covering everything from getting to know a library's materials to marketing and promoting readers' advisory, this practical handbook will help you expand services immediately without adding costs or training time.

The Readers' Advisory Guide to Genre Fiction, Second Edition. Provocative and spirited, this new edition offers hands-on strategies for librarians who want to become experts at figuring out what their readers are seeking and how to match books with those interests.